International Labour Office
Regional Office for Asia and the Pacific

Labour and Social Trends in Asia and the Pacific 2005

Bookwell New Delhi

ISBN: 81-89640-12-7

This edition is published in India in 2006 by:

BOOKWELL

Sales Office:

24/4800, Ansari Road, Darya Ganj,
New Delhi-110002
Ph: 91-11-23268786, 23257264.
FAX: 91-11-3281315
E-Mail: bookwell@vsnl.net

Head Office:

2/72, Nirankari Colony,
Delhi-110009. Ph: 91-11-27251283
E-Mail: bkwell@nde.vsnl.net.in

Foreword

Labour and Social Trends in Asia and the Pacific is the first issue of a new report to be published every second year. The report has two main aims, the first of which is to present major trends in employment and social conditions in the world's most populous and dynamic region, while also drawing attention to key policy challenges posed by the identified trends.

The second aim of the report is to contribute to the development of internationally comparable, gender-sensitive indicators to measure progress in decent work. Decent work is a goal, meaning not just whether women and men have any job, but productive employment that provides: an adequate income to keep them and their families out of poverty, security in times of adversity, good working conditions and a voice in decisions that affect their lives and livelihoods. To identify decent work gaps, and measure progress made in the different dimensions of decent work – many of which are of a fundamentally qualitative nature – it is crucial to have relevant and up-to-date information.

The report uses data from the ILO and other sources. The data problems encountered are several: missing data for countries and years, lack of comparability across countries and over time, questionable data values, data from different sources showing substantially different patterns and, fundamentally, that data do not exist that adequately address the underlying concept one wants to know about. The present report highlights information gaps and suggests improvements in data collection. This is part of an ILO initiative to establish a regional Decent Work Indicator database and provide technical advice and support to countries to develop national data compilation capacity.

The report is the result of strong collaboration between the ILO Regional, Subregional and Country Offices in Asia and the Pacific and various ILO units at Headquarters in Geneva through the Task Force on Decent Work Indicators for the Asia-Pacific Region. The Task Force comprises members from the Regional and Subregional Offices and also Headquarters staff from the Policy Integration Department, Employment Strategy Department, Bureau of Statistics and the International Institute for Labour Studies. The main objective of the Task Force was to facilitate the work of the ILO in the region in respect of helping countries to move forward on implementing the Decent Work Agenda, and to oversee the establishment of a regional statistical database on decent work indicators that eventually covers all countries and is updated regularly.

Special acknowledgement and thanks go to the Statistical Development and Analysis Group of the Policy Integration Department (Geneva) for their valuable technical contribution; to Peter Peek, Chief of the Unit, for coordinating the work in the first phase, to David Kucera for preparing the first draft of the report, and to Anne Chataignier and Sudip Ranjan Basu for compiling the data base. The contributions from a number of colleagues of the ILO Subregional Offices and Country Offices in Asia and the Pacific were essential in the identification and evaluation of the employment and social trends presented in the report. The valuable cooperation of the Employment Trends Team of the Employment Strategy Department (Geneva) is also gratefully acknowledged; they provided access to the latest ILO data and their comments and suggestions on the draft manuscript have greatly helped in preparing and refining the report.

The final version of the report was prepared by the Economic and Social Analysis Unit of the ILO Regional Office for Asia and the Pacific, with Gyorgy Sziraczki having the primary responsibility for the report. Valuable inputs were provided by many colleagues: Urmila Sarkar, Kenta Goto and Yukiko Arai contributed to different sections; and Somsward Punkrasin provided research and secretarial support. Special mention should be given to Bijoy Raychaudhuri who, in addition to extensively contributing to the analytical parts of the report, was also responsible for the statistical annex, and to Lin Lean Lim, Deputy Regional Director, who coordinated the work related to the report and provided key technical contributions.

I believe this report will be useful to people interested in labour and social issues, and helpful to all in pursuit of decent work in the region.

Shinichi Hasegawa
Regional Director
Regional Office for Asia and the Pacific

Contents

Contents *(continued)*

Page

List of Figures

List of Tables

Acronyms and Abbreviations

ADB	Asian Development Bank
ARM	Asian Regional Meeting
ASEAN	Association of South-East Asian Nations
DWI	Decent Work Indicators
FDI	Foreign direct investment
GDP	Gross domestic product
ICT	Information and communication technology
ILC	International Labour Conference
IR	Industrial relations
IT	Information technology
ITES	Information technology enabled services
LMI	Labour market information
MDG	Millennium Development Goal
MNEs	Multinational enterprises
PRSP	Poverty Reduction Strategy Papers
SIMPOC	Statistical Information and Monitoring Programme on Child Labour
SMEs	Small and medium-sized enterprises
UNDP	United Nations Development Programme
UNESCAP	United Nations Economic and Social Commission for Asia and the Pacific
UNESCO	United Nations Education, Scientific and Cultural Organization
UNICEF	United Nations Children's Fund

1

Overview

Asia and the Pacific most economically dynamic region in the world

Recent economic growth in Asia and the Pacific, which is home to more than four billion people, has been by far the most rapid in the world. In recent years, the region has grown at a rate over twice the world average and is projected to continue outpacing the rest of the world in coming years. Its dynamism has been manifested not only by its rate of economic growth but also by its rapid and competitive integration into global markets for goods, services and investment. Asia has had exceptional export performance compared to other regions of the world. Intra-Asian trade has been growing much faster than trade with the rest of the world. Many Asian countries are now trading more between themselves than with other non-Asian markets – reflecting both the rising importance of Asian consumers and the growing involvement of Asian countries in different stages of global production systems. The region houses major global production systems operated by multinational enterprises.

Asia is the biggest destination in the developing world for foreign direct investment (FDI), with more and more of these flows originating within the region. Asia is also the largest and fastest growing outward investor, accounting for three-quarters of the total outward FDI stock of developing economies and four-fifths of total outflows during 2002-2003.[1] It accounts for nearly 90 per cent of net portfolio equity flows to emerging markets and has the highest level of savings, along with the largest accumulation of foreign reserves, in the world.[2]

Great diversity and imbalances within the region

There is great diversity within Asia and the Pacific – from the developed, industrialized economies (Japan, Australia and New Zealand) to the previous "Asian miracle economies" (the "tigers" – Hong Kong (China), Republic of Korea, Singapore and Taiwan, China; and the "tiger cubs" – Indonesia, Malaysia, the Philippines, Thailand) to the least developed countries (Afghanistan, Bangladesh, Cambodia, Kiribati, Lao PDR, Myanmar, Nepal, Papua New Guinea, Samoa, Solomon Islands, Timor-Leste and Vanuatu). Several countries have remained mired in social conflicts and other tensions, with the path to economic and social development as well as democracy hampered by the lack of decent and productive employment opportunities for the population.

Total number of unemployed has been climbing

Despite strong economic growth in Asia, recent trends show the labour market situation largely unchanged in 2004. Unemployment edged up by half a million from 2003, reaching 73.8 million in 2004 (Table 1), according to ILO estimates.[3] This

[1] UNCTAD, *World Investment Report 2004: The Shift Towards Services,* (New York and Geneva, 2004).

[2] UNESCAP, *Meeting the Challenges in an Era of Globalization by Strengthening Regional Development Cooperation* (New York, United Nations, 2004).

[3] ILO, *Key Indicators of the Labour Market (4th Edition),* (Geneva, ILO, 2005) (forthcoming).

Table 1: Unemployment, employment and labour force in Asia and the Pacific, 1999, 2003-2004 (millions)

	1999	2003	2004
Unemployment	66.4	73.3	73.8
Employment	1 471.7	1 562.8	1 587.9
Labour force	1 538.1	1 636.1	1 661.7

Source: ILO, *Key Indicators of the Labour Market* (4th edition), (Geneva, ILO, 2005) (forthcoming).

increase marked the fifth consecutive year since 1999 that the year-over-year number of unemployed had increased. The unemployment rate was marginally down in East Asia (from 3.7 per cent in 2003 to 3.6 per cent in 2004) and South-East Asia (from 6.3 per cent in 2003 to 6.2 per cent in 2004), but stayed unchanged in South Asia (4.8 per cent). But the Asia-Pacific unemployment rates shown in Table 2 are still the lowest among regions in the world.

Table 2: Labour market indicators in Asia and the Pacific, 1999, 2003-2004

	Unemployment rate (%)		Employment growth rate (%)	GDP growth rate (%)		Labour force participation rate (%)		Annual labour force growth rate (%)
	2003	2004	2004	2003	2004	1999	2004	1999-2004
East Asia	3.7	3.6	1.0	6.7	7.8	77.1	75.0	0.9
South-East Asia	6.3	6.2	2.0	5.0	6.3	70.3	70.2	2.2
South Asia	4.8	4.8	2.3	7.8	6.4	60.5	60.0	2.3
Total	4.5	4.4	1.6	6.7*	7.3*	69.6	68.3	1.6

* Average, including Central Asia.

Sources: ILO, *Key Indicators of the Labour Market* (4th edition) (Geneva, ILO, 2005) (forthcoming); and Asian Development Bank, *Asian Development Outlook 2005 Promoting Competition for Long-term Development* (Hong Kong, China, ADB, 2005) (GDP data).

Youth hardest hit by rising unemployment

Young women and men aged 15-24 years bore the brunt of rising unemployment. While young people made up 20.8 per cent of Asia's labour force in 2004, unemployed youth constituted 49.1 per cent – almost half – of the region's total jobless population. The youth unemployment rate stood at 7.5 per cent in East Asia, 10.8 per cent in South Asia and a staggering 17.1 per cent in South-East Asia including the Pacific island states. Except in Singapore where the ratio of youth to adult unemployment rates was close to parity, other countries for which data is available show youth unemployment at least twice to three times as high as adult unemployment. Among young people, women have higher unemployment rates than men in South-East Asia and South Asia.

The ILO has estimated that halving youth unemployment would increase GDP by between 1.5 and 2.5 per cent in East Asia, between 4.6 and 7.4 per cent in South-East Asia and between 4.2 and 6.7 per cent in South Asia.

Employment growth has not matched economic growth

Employment in Asia and the Pacific increased from 1,563 billion in 2003 to 1,588 billion in 2004, an increase of 1.6 per cent or 25 million additional jobs. However, in relation to the strong economic growth rate of about 7 per cent, the growth of employment remained disappointing. Employment as a share of the working-age population remained virtually unchanged at 65.3 per cent in 2004.

A closer look at the subregions reveals weak employment growth in East Asia where employment grew by 1 per cent in 2004, despite a GDP growth rate of

7.8 per cent. The poor employment record of East Asia is not a new phenomenon as exemplified by China's deteriorating employment intensity to GDP growth,[4] which means that 1 percentage point economic growth creates fewer jobs today than before. The case of China should, however, be explained more fully. Firstly, low employment elasticity has to be considered in relation to the high GDP growth because GDP growth is the denominator of the employment elasticity measure. Secondly, whether low employment elasticity is indicative of poor employment performance has to be seen in the context of other labour market trends. For example, low employment elasticity is not a problem if unemployment is also low. But China's unemployment rate rose from 2.5 per cent in 1990 to 4.3 per cent in 2003, and the numbers made jobless by the restructuring of state enterprises continue to be huge. At the same time, however, there is evidence of growing labour shortages especially of skilled workers in the special economic zones of China.

The recent relatively low rate of job creation in other countries, such as Indonesia, Pakistan and India, gives cause for concern. The region's labour force is set to continue growing in the coming years, and unless economic growth becomes more employment-intensive (or there is a significant and sustainable improvement in growth) the prospects of denting into the number of unemployed and absorbing millions of new jobseekers are bleak. Most of the increase in labour force will be in countries with the highest numbers of working poor and the largest informal economies. The bulk of new entrants into the labour force will occur in China, India, Indonesia, Bangladesh, Pakistan and other large populous Asian countries.

Both quantity and quality of jobs matter

Trends in overall employment and unemployment are quantitative indicators but there are critical qualitative dimensions to decent work. In addition to creating new jobs, policy-makers face major challenges to improve employment conditions and the quality of jobs. The challenge is not just to ensure that people have jobs but that their working conditions are safe and healthy, their basic rights are upheld and their work is productive so that they are able to earn enough to keep themselves and their families out of abject poverty.

Informal employment important but data scanty

In this regard, improving working conditions in the informal economy is a major challenge. According to recent estimates, informal employment in developing Asia comprises about 65 per cent of non-agricultural employment, as compared to 48 per cent in North Africa, 51 per cent in Latin America and 72 per cent in Sub-Saharan Africa.

Because of data availability constraints, informal employment is commonly proxied by non-agricultural self-employment as a per cent of total non-agricultural employment. This indicator for the 1990/2000 period was far above the world average in South Asia (50 per cent as compared to 32 per cent), well below the world average in East Asia (18 per cent) and about equal to the world average in South-East Asia (33 per cent).

Self-employment is a larger share (an estimated 59 per cent in Asia) of non-agricultural informal employment than wage employment. For most of the countries for which data exists, non-agricultural self-employment as a percentage of total non-agricultural employment has been on the decline in recent years. However, this

[4] "The total economy employment elasticity to growth decreased from 0.45 in 1989 to 0.10 in 2000", according to ILO, *Global Employment Trends* (Geneva, ILO, 2003), p. 29.

should not be taken to necessarily mean a decline in informality – since informal wage employment may, in fact, be increasing, and working conditions are often poorer in informal wage employment, such as for casual labourers, than in informal self-employment.

Statistics on the informal economy are scanty, especially time series data. Without better statistics the largest segment of the labour force is not adequately measured and fully understood. And without better statistics, it is difficult to monitor and evaluate the impact of policies to promote decent and productive employment in the informal economy.

Progress but not likely to achieve MDG3 on gender equality

A number of indicators show progress over the past 15 years – but there is still a long way to go to close the decent work gaps. The limited available data indicates that gender gaps in literacy rates, labour force participation rates, unemployment rates and wage levels have been reduced in several countries. Significantly, female labour force participation rates have been increasing fastest in those countries with the largest gender differentials – so that there seems to be some move towards equality. In a few countries, namely the more industrialized ones, the gap between male and female manufacturing wages has narrowed slightly.

But overall, women workers still remain disadvantaged and discriminated against, so that many countries, especially in South Asia, are not likely to meet the third Millennium Development Goal (MDG3) on gender equality and empowerment of women. One indicator for MDG3 specified as the female share of non-agricultural wage employment shows that women in South Asia still hold only about 20 per cent of paying jobs outside agriculture. Another indicator based on the ratio of girls to boys in education shows better progress towards the education component rather than the employment component of MDG3. Both East Asia and South-East Asia and the Pacific subregions have made steady progress towards achieving universal primary education and gender parity at the primary school level. At the same time, however, several countries in the region particularly in South Asia will be missing the MDG target on achieving gender parity in primary and secondary education by 2015.

Rising real manufacturing wages but working hours remain long

There have been sizeable increases in real manufacturing wages, in particular in those countries that are major exporters. Very strikingly, real manufacturing wages in China have more than doubled since 1990, and in some other export-oriented East and South-East Asian countries they have increased between 60 to 80 per cent.

At the same time, however, economic growth and productivity gains have not translated into shorter working hours. Workers in developing Asia still work longer hours than most of their counterparts in the world. The top six economies in the world in terms of annual hours worked are all Asian. The long working time is also reflected in the large share of people working 50 hours or more a week out of the total employed. In the Republic of Korea, Mongolia, Cambodia, Singapore, Thailand and Pakistan more than 35 per cent of the employed work 50 hours or more per week.

Substantial progress in reaching MDG1 but problem of working poor remains serious

Countries of Asia and the Pacific have made huge strides in reducing poverty, most remarkably in East and South-East Asia, and the assessment is positive that the region will be able by 2015 to achieve MDG1 to halve the proportion of people living on less than US$1 a day. Yet the region is still home to some 690 million people, more than two-thirds of the world's poor, living on less than US$1 a day. If the poverty line is raised to US$2 a day, Asia has 2 billion poor people or more than three-fourths of the world's poor. The largest number of poor people lives in South Asia. The poverty rate is particularly high in Nepal, Bangladesh and India.

In addition to poverty on a per capita basis, it is critical to examine poverty among workers – the concept of "working poverty". In Asia and the Pacific, many people are working – and working very hard and long hours – but not earning enough to keep themselves or members of their family above the poverty line. The proportion of employed persons living in a household whose members are estimated to be below the US$1 a day poverty line in 2004 was 11 per cent in South-East Asia, 16 per cent in East Asia and 36 per cent in South Asia. Taking the US$2 a day poverty line, the proportion of the working poor rose to 47 per cent in East Asia, 58 per cent in South-East Asia, and a shocking 87 per cent in South Asia.

Uneven decline in child labour across the region

Based on currently available data, in every country in the region the proportion of children aged 10-14 years in the labour force is smaller today than in 1990. Still, the uneven decline across subregions and countries mirrors the uneven reduction in poverty. In Nepal, for example, over 40 per cent of the children aged 10-14 years are still in the labour force and in Timor-Leste more than 35 per cent are working. In several other countries more than 20 per cent of children work.

Asia still has the largest number of child workers in the 5-14 age group – some 127 million, about 60 per cent of working children in the world. At too young an age, these children work long hours, often every day of the week, in mines, in agriculture, in construction and in brick kilns, in fisheries and car repair workshops, in homes and entertainment businesses. Child labour needs to be more adequately measured and better understood considering the hidden and often clandestine nature of child labour including in its worst forms.

Progress towards achieving MDG2 has slowed

The progressive elimination of child labour is inextricably linked to MDG2 to achieve universal primary education by 2015. Despite the progress in enrolment made throughout the 1990s in the region, large numbers of children of primary school age are still not enrolled. In 2001, 103 million children of primary school age were not enrolled in school globally. Of these out-of-school children, 48 million were in this region, with 36 million in South Asia, the majority of who were working.[5]

Trade union density low and declining

Social dialogue plays a pivotal role in balancing economic objectives with social goals. But regardless of the workplace and the country, it is difficult for workers to make their voice heard, partly because freedom of association and the right to organize and to bargain collectively are still problematic in many countries. The level of unionization (union membership as a percentage of the labour force) in Asia and the Pacific is low (only between 3 and 8 per cent in countries such as Bangladesh, Thailand, Malaysia and the Republic of Korea; the highest is about 17 to 18 per cent in New Zealand, Australia and Singapore) and declining. Employers' organizations have also been experiencing formidable challenges including the increasing diversity of companies and the growing presence of multinational firms, which are often outside of their membership.

[5] UNESCO, *Education for All: The quaıııy imperative: EFA Global Monitoring Report 2005* (Paris, UNESCO, 2004), p. 95.

2

Subregional trends in the labour market

The subregional data presented in this chapter[6] refers to the following country groupings:

East Asia	China, Democratic People's Republic of Korea, Hong Kong (China), Macau (China), Mongolia, Republic of Korea and Taiwan (China)
South-East Asia and the Pacific	Brunei Darussalam, Cambodia, Fiji, Indonesia, Lao People's Democratic Republic, Malaysia, Myanmar, Papua New Guinea, Philippines, Solomon Islands, Singapore, Thailand, Timor-Leste and Viet Nam
South Asia	Afghanistan, Bangladesh, Bhutan, India, Maldives, Nepal, Pakistan, and Sri Lanka

2.1 East Asia

Recent trends

East Asia is the world's most populous region, with China accounting for 97 per cent of its total population. The subregion is also the fastest in terms of economic growth, with an average annual GDP growth rate of more than seven per cent in recent years. This process is driven mainly by China, the largest subregional economy, but the smaller economies have also been performing well. For example, in 2004 Mongolia saw a real output growth of 10.6 per cent,[7] a figure well above the rate of growth in China. Labour productivity has also grown rapidly. Output per person employed in East Asia grew at an annual rate of 5.8 per cent between 1993 and 2003.[8]

However, the strong economic performance in the subregion has not been matched by equally strong job creation (Figure 1). The difference between China, the Republic of Korea and Mongolia is striking. With a 38.8 per cent GDP growth China

[6] The main data source for this chapter is the ILO, *Key Indicators of the Labour Market* (Third Edition, Geneva, ILO, 2003) and (Fourth Edition, Geneva, ILO, 2005, forthcoming). Data on economic (GDP) growth comes from the Asian Development Bank, *Asian Development Outlook 2005 Promoting Competition for Long-term Development* (Hong Kong, China, ADB, 2005). While this chapter draws on the ILO, *Global Employment Trends* (ILO, Geneva, 2004), it presents the most recent data, identifying some new trends and highlighting the diversity in employment performance not only across the subregions but also within each subregion in Asia and the Pacific. Australia, Japan and New Zealand comprise the industrialized countries in the region. They are not covered in this chapter but are included in subsequent chapters – which draw upon a wider set of data sources (identified in the Statistical Annex).

[7] The main reasons for this spectacular output growth are the strong economic growth in neighbouring China as well as the high mineral prices in the world market that pushed up the mineral sector's value added, and thus the GDP. However, per head GDP in Mongolia remains low, the country's economic base is narrow and its manufactured goods do not appear to be competitive on the world market.

[8] See ILO, *World Employment Report 2004-05* (Geneva, ILO, 2005), Figure 1.4a, p. 41.

Figure 1: GDP and employment growth, East Asia, 1999-2003 (%)

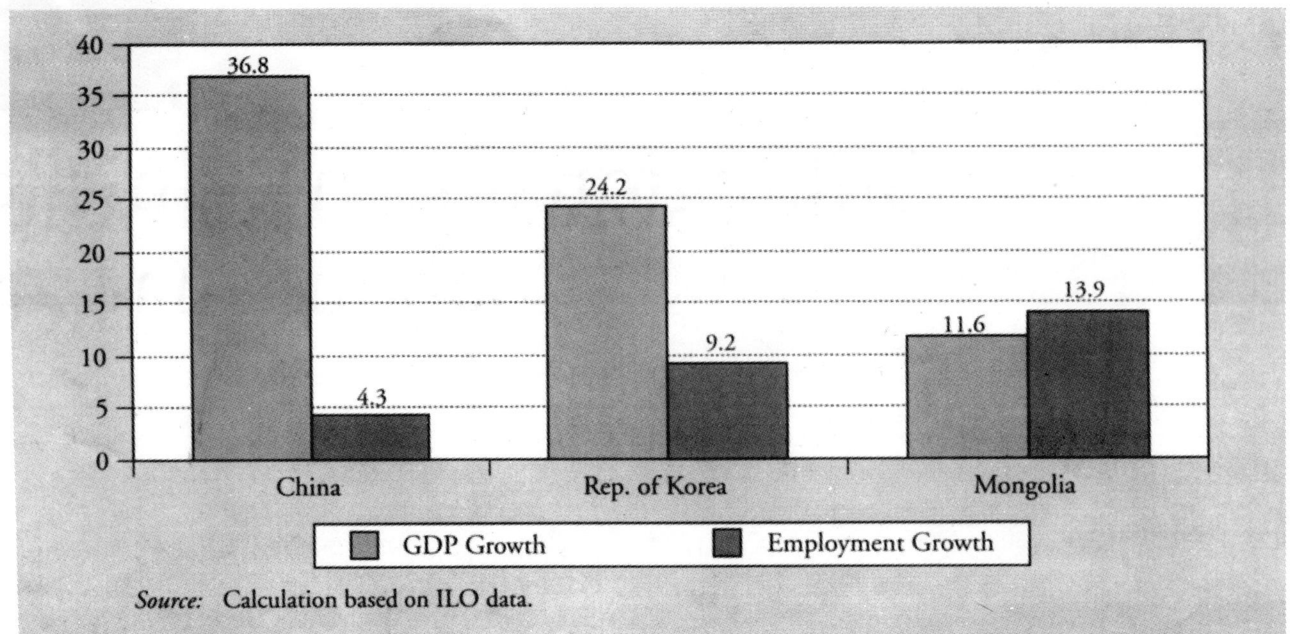

Source: Calculation based on ILO data.

created only 4.3 per cent additional jobs from 1999 to 2003. The Republic of Korea saw a lower rate of GDP growth but a much higher rate of employment growth. And Mongolia, with an even lower rate of real output growth, had the highest rate of job growth in the region.

The low labour absorption in China reflects in part a long-term structural change from employment-intensive growth towards capital-intensive growth, especially in industry. The total economy employment elasticity to growth has decreased over the past 15 years,[9] which means that a 1 percentage point GDP growth creates fewer jobs today than before.

While the employment performance of Mongolia has been spectacular, the fact that the rate of job creation was higher than the rate of GDP growth raises questions about job quality and labour productivity.

Unemployment figures reflect the job creation performance of the countries. China's unemployment rate climbed from 2.5 per cent in 1990 to 3.1 per cent in 2000 to 4.3 per cent in 2003, while rates declined in Mongolia and the Republic of Korea.

Employment and unemployment trends are not only influenced by economic growth, but also by growth in the labour force. The East Asian region has the lowest labour force growth rate in developing Asia, with an average annual growth rate of 0.9 per cent. This low rate stems primarily from a major slowdown in population growth in China and the Republic of Korea, even though the labour force in Mongolia has continued to rapidly expand.

It is important to note that along with increasing unemployment, labour shortages have recently emerged in China and labour costs are rising. In the more industrialized Republic of Korea, labour-intensive industries such as clothing, footwear and toys have almost disappeared because wages are high enough in US dollar terms to render the Republic of Korea uncompetitive as a base for labour-intensive export-oriented manufacturing, especially since the financial crisis of 1997/98. At the same time, capital-intensive and sophisticated engineering exports have grown. Perhaps this dramatic restructuring is one of the main reasons why employment growth in the Republic of Korea (and in other countries such as Singapore and Taiwan, China) has been weak since the late 1990s.

Overall, labour force participation (the proportion of the working-age population that is working or looking for work) in East Asia is high; the rate is just below 80 per cent both in China and

[9] "The total economy employment elasticity to growth decreased from 0.45 in 1989 to 0.10 in 2000", according to ILO, *Global Employment Trends* (Geneva, ILO, 2003), p. 29. The figure for 2004 was 0.12, based on national employment data and GDP data from the ADB.

Mongolia and close to 70 per cent in the Republic of Korea. The labour force participation rate has been declining in China, but rising in the other two countries. Women's labour force participation rates are lower than men's in all three economies though the gender gap is small and slowly closing.

Employment outlook

The East Asian economies are expected to continue to grow almost as rapidly as they have been doing over the last few years. This growth is led by interregional as well as intraregional trade, making the subregion less dependent on world demand than other subregions. The emerging middle-class in China is an increasingly important factor in domestic demand. But risk factors that could affect the growth performance include high oil prices; incomplete yet needed corporate restructuring and banking reforms; problems with public as well as corporate governance and slow infrastructure development, especially in rural areas.

Labour force growth in East Asia is projected to slow down to 0.7 per cent per annum from 2005 to 2015. The main cause will be slower population growth in China, but it will decrease in all economies in the subregion, including Mongolia. The total number of new entrants to the labour force will nevertheless be high, projected at around 60 million until 2015 (over six million new entrants each year).[10]

The key question is whether this overall positive precondition will translate into improvements in the labour market? China has seen a tremendous slowdown in the number of jobs being created compared to GDP growth in recent years due to structural changes and labour shedding in overstaffed state-owned enterprises (an estimated 30 million job losses). Given the steady increase in unemployment, ensuring job creation accompanies economic growth needs to be placed at the forefront of the policy debate. Simultaneously, the emerging labour shortages in skilled workers indicate that the challenge is not only the quantity of jobs but also the quality of jobs (Box 1).

[10] ILO, *Global Employment Trends,* (Geneva, ILO, 2004).

2.2 South-East Asia and the Pacific

Recent trends

South-East Asia has experienced slower economic growth since 1999 than before the financial crisis of 1997/98, although some recent improvements have been observed. Cambodia and Viet Nam have been the best subregional performers since 1999, with annual average GDP growth rates of 7.3 and 6.5 per cent, respectively. On the other hand, output growth has remained under 5.0 per cent in Singapore, Thailand and the Philippines, and under 4.0 per cent in Indonesia, the subregion's largest economy.

Employment growth since 1999 has been strongest in Malaysia and the Philippines, but disappointingly low in Indonesia. The three countries had similar GDP growth, but employment creation in Indonesia remained a fraction of those in the other countries (Figure 2). Not surprisingly, unemployment in Indonesia rose sharply from 6.4 per cent in 1999 to 9.6 per cent in 2004, largely because GDP growth (particularly in manufacturing) was insufficient to create enough jobs to absorb the estimated 2.0 to 2.5 million annual new entrants to the labour market. Simultaneously, unemployment in the Philippines increased modestly, while Malaysia showed little change. But everywhere in South-East Asia the unemployment rate was higher in 2004 than in 1996, indicating that the subregion's employment performance has been weak in recent years.

Underemployment rates[11] are alarming, notably in Indonesia and the Philippines, where the relative number of working poor remains high. During the financial crisis this rate increased (albeit in varying degrees) in all economies in the subregion. Since then, there have been declines in many

[11] The international definition of time-related underemployment, adopted in 1982 by the 13th International Conference of Labour Statisticians, includes all persons in employment "involuntarily working less than the normal duration of work determined for the activity, who were seeking or available for additional work during the reference period". However, few countries have applied the definition consistently and have collected data on a regular basis. Therefore, the share of workers working less than 35 hours a week out of the total employment is used here as a proxy for measuring underemployment.

Box 1: Labour shortage and rising costs: Is China losing its competitiveness?

Can China – population 1.3 billion – really be running out of workers? In many of the most important parts of its booming economy, the answer, increasingly, is yes. In southeast China, it is estimated that there is a labour shortage of 2 million. The shortage is fast affecting the image of China as a source of cheap labour and threatening the export processing zones along the coast that have been the foundation for global production. Firms in the south are complaining that they cannot recruit enough cheap factory and manual workers. The situation is expected to get worse as the demographic transition proceeds faster on the one hand, and, on the other hand, if factories keep opening at the current breakneck pace.

These shortages have pushed up minimum wages to levels equivalent to those in Thailand and way above levels in Bangladesh, Vietnam, Cambodia and Indonesia. Chinese workers in a sneaker factory earn 30 per cent more than their counterparts in Vietnam and 15 per cent more than in Indonesia. In addition to wage increases, companies in China are offering a wide range of supplemental benefits to retain workers. Other large companies are moving production to lower cost countries such as Vietnam or inland in China where labour is cheaper. The rising costs are leading to growing concerns over how China can maintain a competitive position in global production systems.

The reasons behind the labour shortages are worth noting. Very significantly, the shortages are linked to the lack of specific skills and training – so that experienced skilled workers are able to strongly leverage job offers. For every experienced skilled worker, there are 88 vacancies and for every factory technician there are 16 vacancies. A related reason is that factories have not invested in the training of workers – "there is a practice of using workers but not developing them" – mainly because they do not expect the workers, who are migrants from rural areas, to stay long with the company (on average 2.1 years before moving on to other jobs).

The structure of special economic zones in the coastal areas supplied by migrant labour is increasingly difficult to sustain. Although there are still plenty of underemployed workers in the countryside, they are increasingly realistic about the "migrant dream" (in part because of the rapid spread of ICT) and less willing to travel thousands of kilometres to be far away from their families and to work very long hours in monotonous jobs.

The market is even tighter for skilled labour and executive talent. Skilled workers and technicians are taking advantage of acute shortages to demand double-digit salary increases. One in ten executives in Shenzhen and one in 12 in Beijing changed jobs last year. Recruitment, retention and localization of staff are now top of the agenda for many firms in China.

Source: T. Fuller, "Costs rise in China amid labor shortage", *International Herald Tribune,* Wednesday, April 20, 2005, pp. 1 and 10; T. Fuller, "Shoemaker, its workers and today's global labor", *International Herald Tribune,* Wednesday, April 20, 2005, p. 13; "The cost of doing business in China", *The Economist,* 16 April 2005.

Figure 2: GDP and employment growth, South-East Asia, 1999-2003 (%)

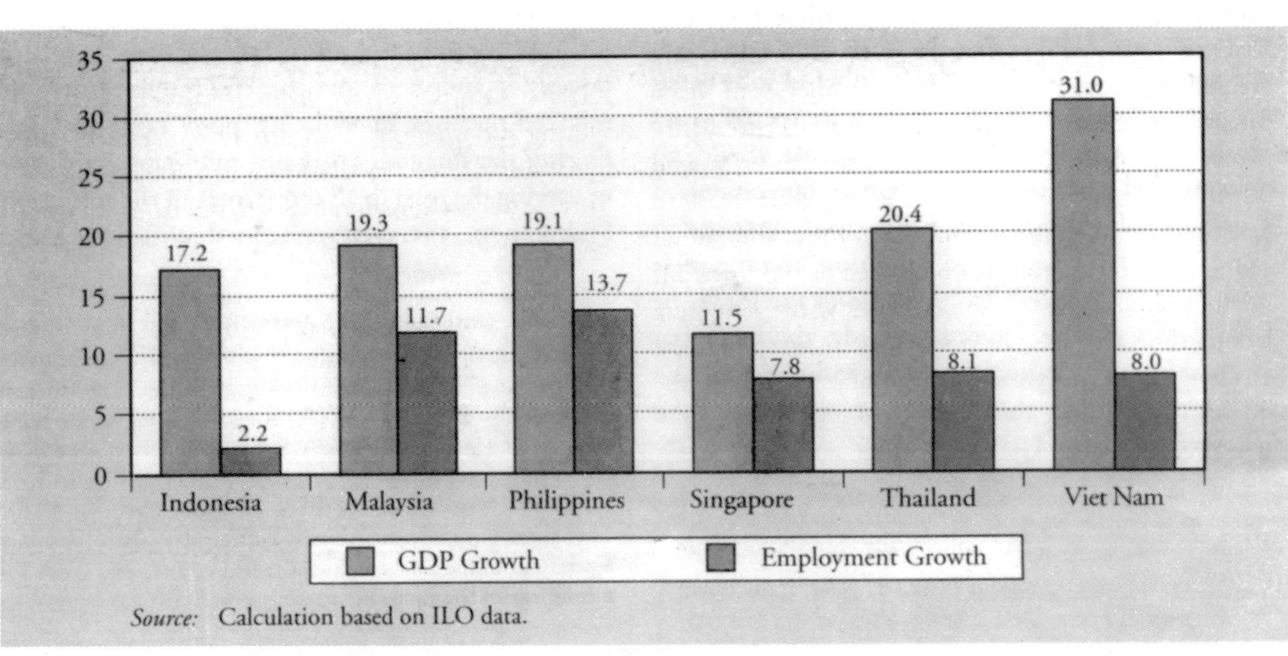

Source: Calculation based on ILO data.

countries though the size of the problem remains a serious concern. In Indonesia, for example, a total of 31.4 million workers in 2002 (or 34.3 per cent of the labour force) were underemployed (working less than 35 hours a week) compared with 34.1 million in 1996, according to Labour Force Survey data.

One reason for the poor labour market performance over the past few years is that some economies still have not recovered from the Asian financial crisis. This is especially true for Indonesia, the biggest economy in the subregion. Another reason for the adverse labour market trends might be that state-owned enterprises in Cambodia and Viet Nam are still releasing a great number of workers. Equally important is the subregion's high labour force growth rate at 2.2 per cent per year, resulting from high population growth rates and rising labour force participation rates. Moreover, due to internal migration, the urban labour force is growing faster than the rural one, putting pressure on urban labour markets. It is worth noting that the South-East Asian labour markets vary considerably (Table 3), demonstrating their different abilities to create employment.

The Pacific subregion has experienced the poorest economic performance in Asia, adding to its increased marginalization in recent years. In 2004, GDP grew at 2.6 per cent in the Pacific (the best year in the subregion since 2000), which compares with a growth rate of 7.3 per cent in Asia as a whole. Most Pacific island economies have a narrow production base and are vulnerable to external shocks. Poor economic performance, combined with high population and labour force growth, has led to declining living standards and a deteriorating employment situation in many Pacific countries.

Papua New Guinea illustrates the enormous challenge. Its economy grew by 2.5 per cent in 2003, only the second year of growth since 1996. The economy was only marginally larger in 2003 than it had been in 1994, though in the same period the population increased about 25 per cent, or 1 million people. In real terms, GDP per head has fallen 20 per cent in the past decade. The country has fertile agricultural land, extensive forestry and fishery resources, and substantial gold, copper and other mineral resource deposits, as well as reserves of oil and natural gas. But the vast majority of Papua New Guineans work in the informal economy; they are engaged in growing food crops for subsistence consumption or sale in nearby urban informal markets. The capital intensive mining industry (the country's strongest sector) makes a relatively small contribution to employment growth.

Table 3: Labour market indicators, selected countries in South-East Asia

	Unemployment rate (%)				Labour force participation rate, latest year, (%)			Employ-ment-to-population ratio, latest year
	1996	1999	2003	2004	Total	Male	Female	
Cambodia	...	...	3.5	3.1	84.0	84.2	83.9	70.4
Indonesia	4.0	6.4	9.1	9.6	71.2	84.5	57.8	61.7
Lao PDR	...	...	...	...	83.9	90.3	77.7	...
Malaysia	2.5	3.4	3.6	3.5	66.5	82.0	50.7	59.8
Myanmar	...	...	...	...	78.9	89.5	68.4	59.8
Philippines	7.4	9.6	11.4	11.8	66.9	82.6	51.1	...
Singapore	3.0	4.6	5.4	4.0	69.7	83.6	55.3	61.0
Timor-Leste	...	...	...	...	82.3	85.8	76.3	...
Thailand	1.1	3.0	1.5	2.1	83.8	89.7	78.0	72.6
Viet Nam	2.7	...	5.8	5.6	81.4	84.5	78.3	73.2

Source: Statistical Annex; and Asian Development Bank, *Asian Development Outlook 2005 Promoting Competition for Long-term Development* (Hong Kong, China, ADB, 2005).

Employment outlook

South-East Asia has been confronting a phase of volatility and uncertainty in the world economy since recovering from the 1997/98 financial crisis. It has managed to navigate through this period reasonably well in terms of economic growth rates. Some of this success has translated into employment gains, but the overall labour market performance has not matched the success before the financial crisis. In the Pacific, the economic and employment outlook depends on political stability in the countries, investment and growth in key sectors as well as the external environment.

Slowing labour force growth rates will take some pressures off South-East Asia's labour markets. Labour force growth rates are expected to slow down to 1.8 per cent annually between 2005 and 2015, compared with 2.2 per cent annually between 1999 and 2004. Nevertheless, between 2005 and 2015, more than 5 million people will enter the subregion's labour market each year.[12] This is nearly the same as in the 1990s when the subregion did well in terms of growth and reducing the number of working poor. Even if success in reducing the working poor rate can be repeated, the South-East Asian countries need to create new employment opportunities to avoid stagnation in unemployment rates in the future. This is especially relevant for Indonesia given its high unemployment and underemployment rates.

[12] ILO, *Global Employment Trends,* (Geneva, ILO, 2004).

2.3 South Asia

Recent trends

South Asia has had solid economic growth in recent years, though slower than in the past decade. Since 1999, the Indian economy has grown by 5.9 per cent per year. Bangladesh and the Islamic Republic of Iran[13] had real output growth rates of above 5 per cent, while Nepal, Pakistan and Sri Lanka have grown at an annual average of between 3.7 and 4.0 per cent.

The estimated employment growth has been stronger in Sri Lanka but weaker in India and especially in Pakistan (Figure 3). These trends are confirmed by unemployment figures. The latest available figures show that the unemployment rate in Sri Lanka declined from 11.3 per cent in 1996 to 8.4 per cent in 2004, whereas it increased in India from 2.2 per cent in 1995 to 4.3 per cent in 2000 and in Pakistan from 5.4 in 1996 to 8.3 per cent in 2003. The unemployment rate also increased in Bangladesh.

[13] Although not part of the South Asian subregional data set, employment trends in the Islamic Republic of Iran are highlighted in this section as the country is covered by the ILO Subregional Office for South Asia.

Figure 3: GDP and employment growth, South Asia, 1999-2003 (%)

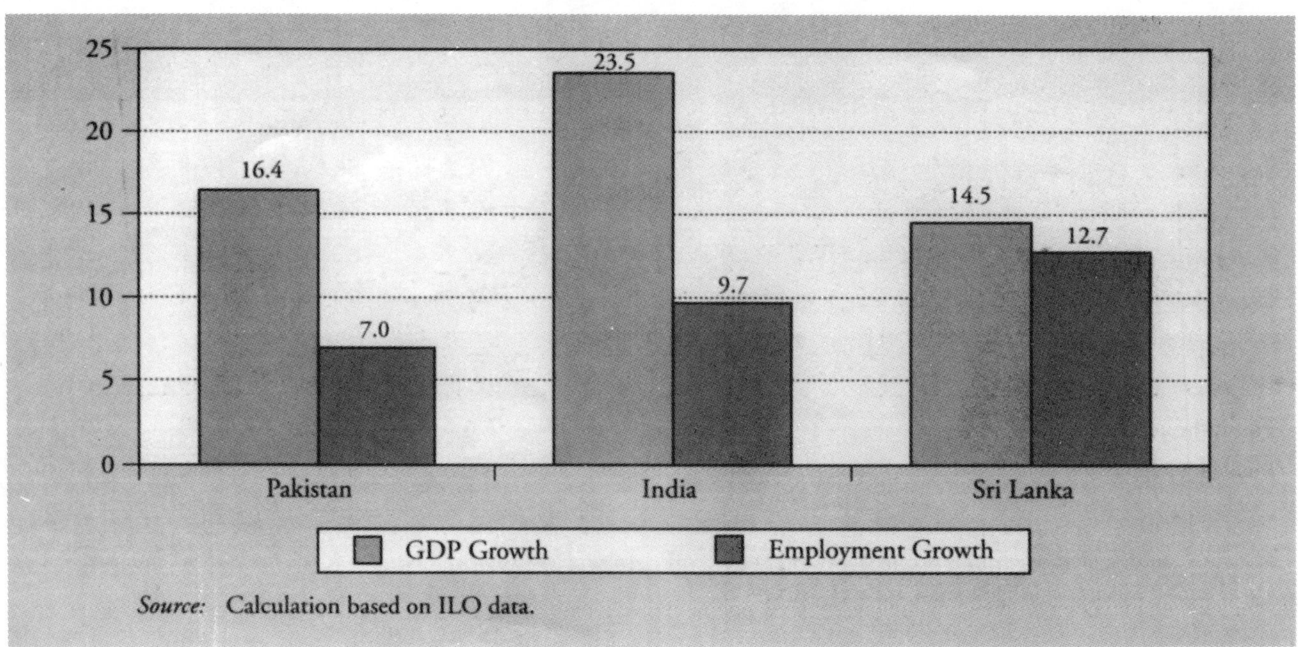

Source: Calculation based on ILO data.

The South Asian employment-to-population ratio of about 57 per cent is one of the lowest in the world; only Central and Eastern Europe (non-European Union) and the Middle-East and North Africa regions have a lower ratio. Employment-to-population ratios (the share of people with work among the working age population) moved in the opposite direction of unemployment rates. The decreasing employment-to-population ratios in India, Pakistan and Bangladesh indicate declining demand for workers in these countries. At the same time, the rising unemployment rates show that people are actively, but unsuccessfully, looking for work. These two trends together suggest that employment creation has been unable to absorb the growing labour force.

South Asia's labour force has been growing at a strong annual average of about 2.3 per cent, mainly reflecting high population growth rates but also increasing labour force participation rates, particularly of women. However, labour force participation rates remain low, compared with other subregions in Asia and the Pacific. These low rates are mainly due to the enormous discrepancy between the reported rates for men and women (Figure 4). At the same time, female unemployment rates are generally much higher than male unemployment rates within the subregion, a particularly worrying trend in countries where female labour force participation is still low. Women in these economies have limited employment opportunities and, if employed, generally earn less than their male counterparts.

Another concern in South Asia is the low literacy rate of the adult population. Research has shown that there is a strong relationship between levels of per capita income and adult literacy rates, indicating that skills and education are strongly linked to income levels.[14] Among the developing regions across the globe, South Asia has the lowest adult literacy rate at 55.8 per cent (compared to a world average of 79.1 per cent and 90.2 per cent in the rest of Asia and the Pacific). Bangladesh, Nepal and Pakistan all have adult literacy rates of about 40 per cent and India has a rate of 57.2 per cent. Sri Lanka is the only country in the subregion with a high adult literacy rate.

[14] See David Kucera and Sarna Ritash: "Child labour, education and export performance", Policy Integration Department Working Papers No. 52, (Geneva, ILO, 2004), p. 27.

Figure 4: Labour force participation rates by sex (aged 15-64), South Asia, latest year available (%)

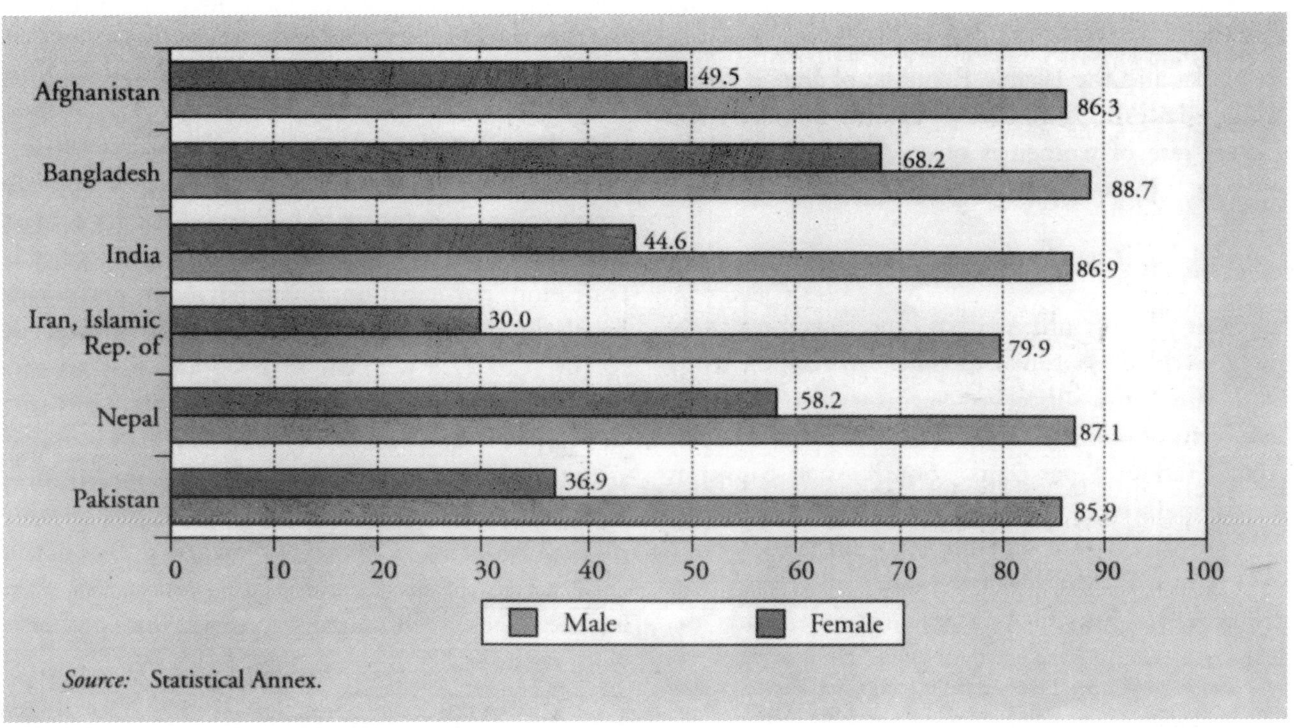

Source: Statistical Annex.

Figure 5: Adult literacy rates by sex, South Asia, latest year available (%)

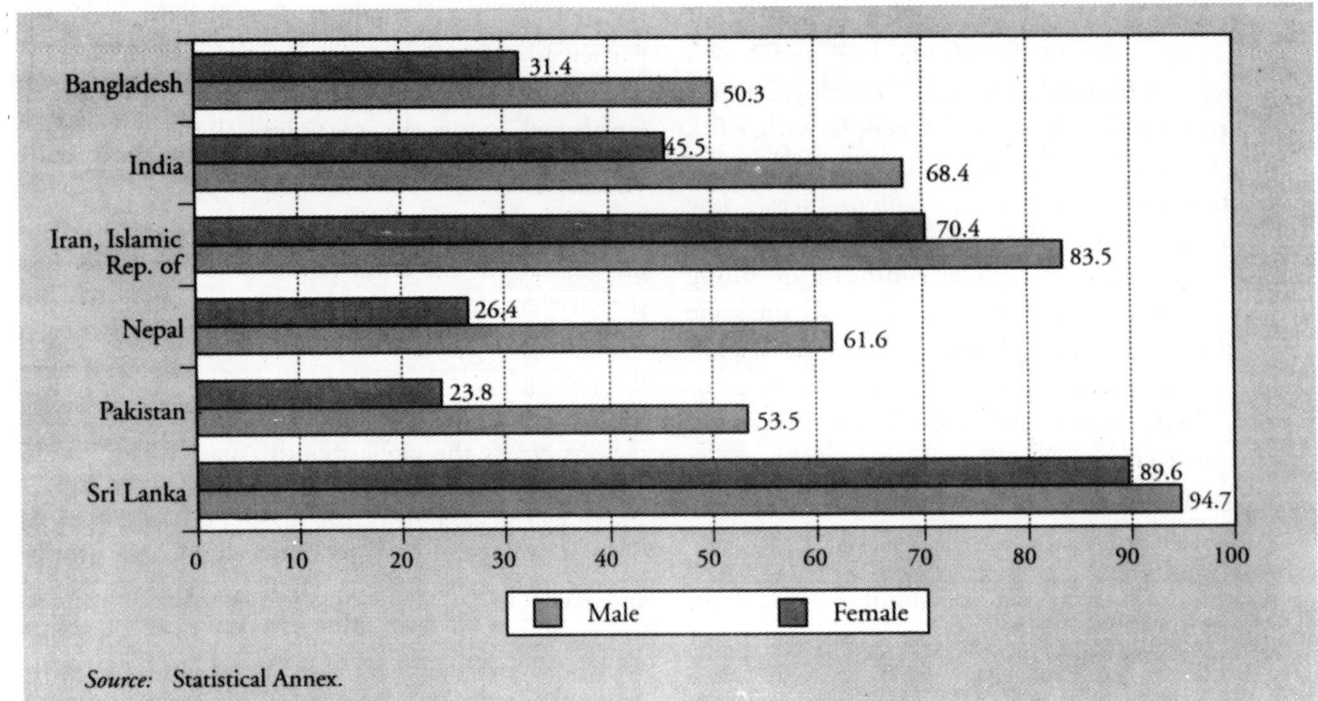

Source: Statistical Annex.

However, it is not only the overall literacy rate that is conducive to economic growth but also greater equality between men and women. Studies on the effect of gender equality in education on economic growth provide evidence that greater gender equality is associated with more rapid growth.[15] In this respect, South Asia does not fare well either. While the gender gap in literacy levels in Sri Lanka and the Islamic Republic of Iran is small, in Bangladesh, Indian, Nepal and Pakistan the literary rate of women is often 40 to 50 per cent lower than those of men (Figure 5).

Employment outlook

In recent years, South Asia has experienced relatively low growth in per capita income. In relation to its population, the subregion accounts for less than 6 per cent of global GDP and an even lower share of exports (about 1 per cent). South Asian countries are comparatively closed to trade and investment: the subregion's ratios of merchandise and service exports to GDP are lower than any other region in the world. South Asia strongly depends on agriculture and therefore on weather conditions and demand for agricultural products. In India, for example, the agricultural sector contributes to one-quarter of GDP and employs about 65 per cent of the labour force.

Overall prospects for the subregion's labour market largely depend on the performance of India, which has a share in the subregional GDP of 80 per cent. The key issues in South Asia include: high levels of unemployment and underemployment; a high incidence of working poverty; low employment generation in high-productivity sectors; low adult literacy rates; and large gender gaps in education, participation, unemployment, and wages. South Asia's GDP growth rate has been stronger in recent years (7.8 per cent in 2003 and 6.4 per cent in 2004), and is forecasted to stay above 5 per cent in the next few years.[16] But the employment situation is not expected to change significantly. The policy challenge is to move from job creation in the informal economy to creating productive employment in the formal sector – otherwise, there is little hope of substantially reducing the number of working poor.

[15] Stephen Klasen: "Does gender inequality reduce growth and development? Evidence from cross-country regressions", World Bank Policy Research Report on Gender and Development, Working Paper Series No. 7, 1999.

[16] Asian Development Bank, *Asian Development Outlook 2005 Promoting Competition for Long-term Development* (Hong Kong, China, ADB, 2005).

The South Asian labour force is projected to grow by more than 2 per cent a year between 2005 and 2015, adding more than 13 million new entrants to the labour market every year. According to ILO estimates,[17] to halve working poverty (220 million working poor live in the region) as well as to halve the unemployment rate by 2015, South Asia would need yearly GDP growth rates of 6.2 per cent, less than 1 percentage point above the growth rate of the past ten years. This gives the subregion a chance to reach the goal but only if the labour market problems mentioned above are addressed.

[17] Steven Kapsos: "Estimating growth requirements for reducing working poverty: Can the world halve working poverty by 2015?", Employment Strategy Papers No. 14 (Geneva, ILO, 2004).

3

Employment, wages and working time

3.1 Employment structure

Rapid economic development in Asia and the Pacific has been accompanied by fundamental changes in the sectoral composition of employment. Over the past 15 years, there has been a marked shift away from agriculture to industry and services, along with population shift from rural to urban areas.

The share of agricultural employment to total employment has shrunk in almost every country between 1990 and the latest year for which data is available (Figure 6). This trend also reflects the declining contribution of agricultural output to GDP. Mongolia is the only country where the share of the agricultural labour force was higher in 2003 than a decade before. But since 1999 the country's labour force share in agriculture has fast been declining.

Despite a decline in agricultural jobs, many workers are still employed in the sector in a number of countries. In Mongolia, Indonesia, Thailand and Pakistan, more than 40 per cent of workers are in the agricultural sector. In China, more than half of the labour force is in agriculture, as is more than 60 per cent of the workforce of Nepal, Cambodia, Viet Nam, India, Bangladesh, Afghanistan, the Philippines and Papua New Guinea (Figure 7). But in a few Pacific countries (Fiji and Kiribati) and in Asia's more developed economies (the Republic of Korea, Singapore, Japan, Australia and New Zealand) less than 10 per cent of the workforce is employed in agriculture.

With the exception of Cambodia, nowhere in Asia and the Pacific has the industrial sector created enough jobs to compensate for large-scale job losses in agriculture. Not even in Malaysia, Indonesia and Thailand, where the share of the industrial workforce increased between 4 to 6 percentage points between 1990-2003. In South Asia, where the contribution of industry to GDP changed little between 1990 and the latest year for which data is available, changes in the share of industrial workforce also remained modest. However, in other Asian countries where the share of industrial output in total GDP declined, employment also dropped sharply. Among these countries, Singapore and the Republic of Korea recorded the largest drops of -11.1 and -7.8 percentage points, respectively. Japan, Australia, New Zealand and Mongolia experienced moderate declines.

The share of industrial employment is the highest (between 30 to 34 per cent) in Fiji, the Islamic Republic of Iran, Japan and the Republic of Korea. The industrial workforce represents 20 to 30 per cent of the total employment in China, Singapore, Thailand, Pakistan, Sri Lanka and the developed (industrialized) economies of Japan, Australia and New Zealand. But Kiribati, Cambodia, Bangladesh and Nepal have a share of about only 10 per cent or less.

The service sector has been the main source of job creation since the early 1990s. The service sector workforce grew most rapidly in countries where the sector's output (measured as a percentage of the GDP) also grew. The share of service employment increased in the Republic of Korea by 16.8 percentage points, in Singapore by 11.1 percentage points, and in the South Asian

Figure 6: Change in the share of agricultural, industry and service employment, 1990-2003 (percentage point change)

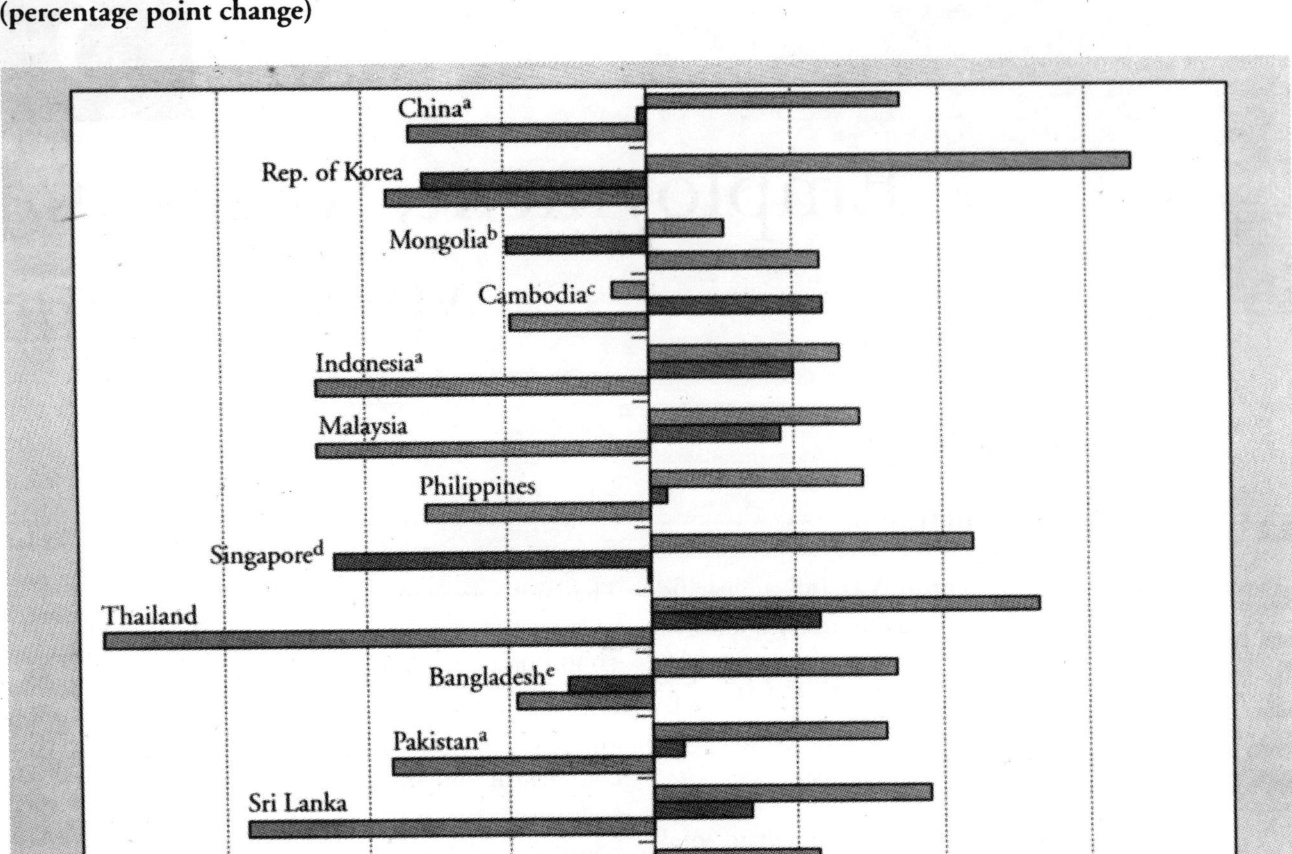

Note: Period covers 1990 to 2003, except for [a] Period covers 1990-2002; [b] Period covers 1993-2003; [c] Period covers 1993-2001; [d] Period covers 1991-2003; [e] Period covers 1990-2000.

Source: Statistical Annex.

countries by 8 to 10 percentage points. Employment in services also expanded in many East and South-East Asian countries (Thailand, China, Indonesia, Malaysia and the Philippines) where the sector's contribution to the GDP remained unchanged, or even declined. Employment in services also grew in Japan, Australia and New Zealand. Again, the only exception is Cambodia, where the share of services in total employment declined.

The share of service employment varies across countries. In Singapore, Australia, Japan, New Zealand, the Republic of Korea and Kiribati, more than 60 per cent of the labour force is in the service sector. In Malaysia, more than half of the labour force is in services, while over 40 per cent of the work force of Mongolia, the Islamic Republic of Iran, the Philippines and Sri Lanka work in the sector. But in China, Cambodia and Viet Nam only around 20 per cent or less of workers are employed in services.

When comparing changes in the composition of production output and employment, three patterns emerge. First, the more developed countries (the Republic of Korea, Singapore, Australia, New Zealand and Japan) have shifted from industry to services. Both output growth and employment

Figure 7: Employment distribution by sector, 2003 or latest year available (%)

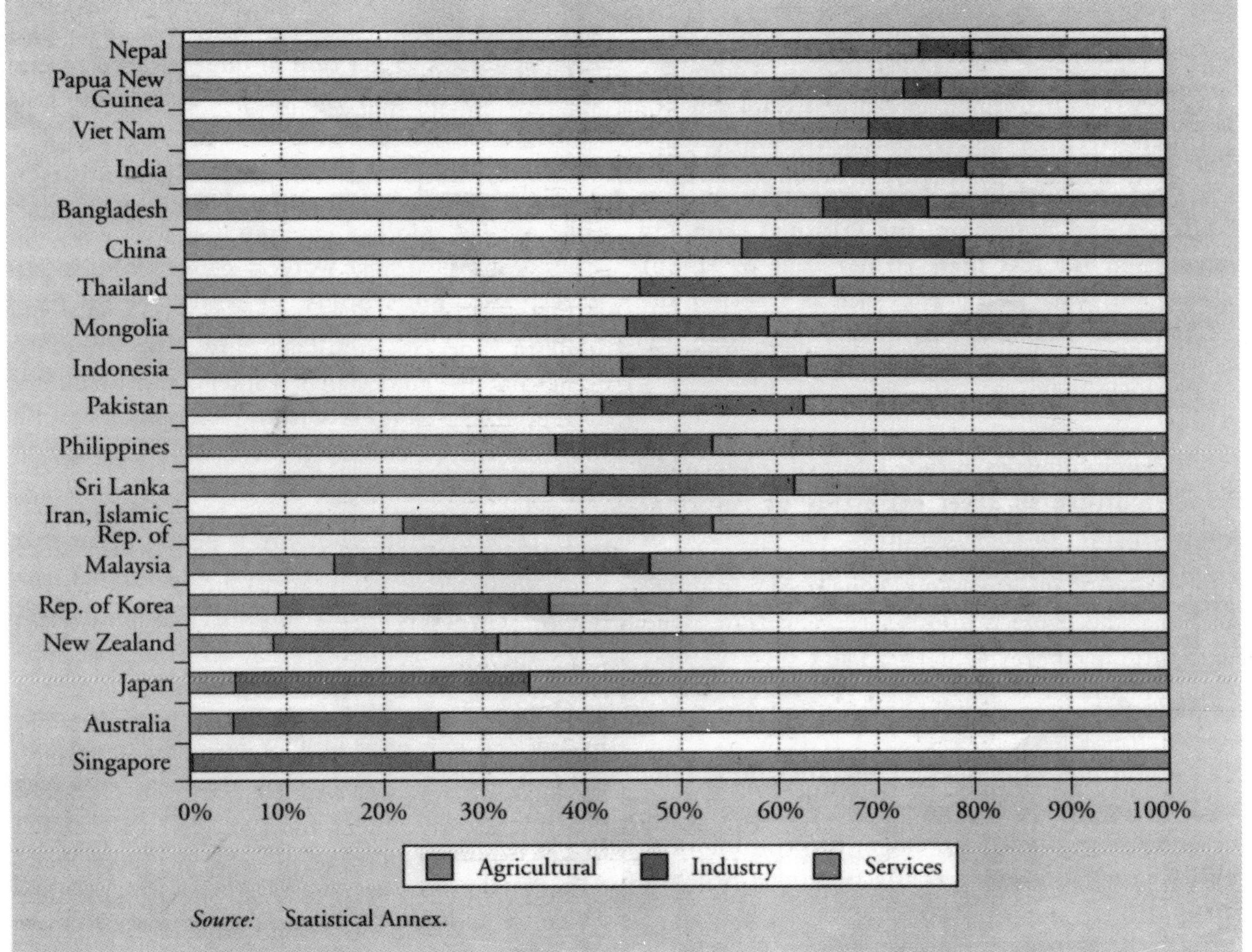

Source: Statistical Annex.

growth have concentrated on the service sector at the expense of the industrial sector.

Second, South Asian countries have experienced a shift away from agriculture towards services, even if they still remain among the most agricultural countries in the world. Both the output growth and the employment growth in the subregion have focused on the service sector at the expense of agriculture.

Third, in some open economies in East and South-East Asia, output growth has been in industry (primarily in manufacturing) but employment growth has been in services. The case of China is particularly telling. The share of its industrial output increased by 9.5 percentage points from 1990 to 2002 but the share of industrial employment fell by -0.3 percentage points. At the same time, the share of service output increased by a mere 1.2 percentage points while the share of service employment jumped by 8.7 percentage points.

It is important to note that the expanding service sector in Asia is remarkably diverse, ranging from street vendors in the informal economy to sophisticated financial service providers. The driving forces behind the growth of the sector as well as its composition vary across countries. There is a need for improved statistics and detailed research to better understand the conditions of work in this expanding sector.

3.2 Informal employment

Only recently have labour statisticians began to capture the informal economy in quantitative terms. Still, there are some problems in defining informal economy employment and statistics often lack comparability.[18]

Available recent estimates[19] show that informal employment in developing Asia comprises about 65 per cent of non-agricultural employment, but there are large differences across countries. In the newly industrializing Asian economies, such as Malaysia and Singapore, the informal economy accounted for less than 10 per cent of labour absorption, while in countries such as Thailand, the Philippines, Indonesia and India it accounted for half to more than three-quarters of non-agricultural employment (Table 4).

Some countries include informal employment in agriculture in their estimates of informal employment. In these countries, the inclusion of informal employment in agriculture increases the proportion of informal employment significantly: in India, the figure is from 83 per cent from non-agricultural employment to 93 per cent of total employment.

Informal employment includes both self-employment in informal enterprises (i.e., small and/or unregistered) and wage employment in informal jobs (i.e., without secure contracts, worker benefits, or social protection). Self-employment is a larger share of non-agricultural informal employment than wage employment. Self-employment in developing Asia represents 59 per cent of informal employment (outside agriculture) and 32 per cent of the total non-agricultural employment.

Informal wage employment comprises employees of informal enterprises as well as various types of informal wage workers who work for formal enterprises, households, or who have no fixed employer. These include casual day labourers, domestic workers, industrial outworkers (notably homeworkers), undeclared workers, and part-time or temporary workers without secure contracts, workers' benefits, or social protection.

The informal economy is highly segmented, by location, sector, and status of employment and, across these segments, by social groups and gender. But most workers in the informal economy share a few things in common: they have unproductive and low-paid jobs that are not recognized or protected by law and that offer little or no social protection, rights at work or representation and voice. Although the links are not always simple,[20] there is no doubt that it is poverty forcing most people in developing Asia to take up unattractive jobs in the informal economy and that low incomes provided by these jobs create a vicious circle of poverty.

In Asia and the Pacific, the proportion of women and men non-agricultural workers in informal employment is about the same. However,

[18] See ILO, *Decent Work and the Informal Economy,* Report VI, International Labour Conference, 90th Session, Geneva, 2002. Also *Guidelines concerning a statistical definition of informal employment endorsed by the Seventeenth International Conference of Labour Statisticians,* November-December 2003.

[19] The source of data presented in this section: *Women and Men in the Informal Economy: A Statistical Picture,* ILO, Geneva, 2002.

[20] ILO, *Decent Work and Informal Economy,* Report VI International Labour Conference 90th Session, 2002.

Table 4: Informal employment in non-agricultural employment, by sex, 2000 or latest available year

	Informal employment as percentage of non-agricultural employment	Women's informal employment as percentage of women's non-agricultural employment	Men's informal employment as percentage of men's non-agricultural employment
India	83	86	83
Indonesia	78	77	78
Philippines	72	73	71
Thailand	51	54	49

Source: ILO, *Women and Men in the Informal Economy: A Statistical Picture,* (Geneva, ILO, 2002).

when it is taken into consideration that women's participation rates are lower than men's, informal employment is generally a larger source of employment for women than men. Certain segments of the informal economy have a women's face: especially street vending (except in societies that restrict women's mobility) and home-based work (including both self-employed and home-workers) which are dominated by women. The recent widespread strategy of firms in the formal economy to subcontract component production to first-, second- and third-tier suppliers may have contributed to link women's home-based labour to the formal production system under informal, flexible employment arrangements. Many of the suppliers at the lower end of global production systems are in micro-enterprises or are home-based in the informal economy.

What has been the impact of recent economic developments, deepening globalization and changing labour markets on the informal economy? Has informal employment expanded? It is difficult to answer these questions because of the lack of statistics, especially time series data, on informal employment. The most comprehensive statistics available on employment in the informal economy relate to self-employment. This data shows that between 1980 and 2000 self-employment as a share of non-agricultural employment declined in East Asia (from 23 to 18 per cent), remained unchanged in South-East Asia (around 33 per cent) and increased in South Asia (from 40 to 50 per cent),[21] with Bangladesh having the highest proportion of self-employed workers in the non-agricultural workforce (Figure 8). In each subregion, the share of self-employed women in the female non-agricultural labour force increased, indicating the growing feminization of this segment of the informal economy.

For most countries of the region for which data exists, non-agricultural self-employment as a percentage of total non-agricultural employment has been on the decline in recent years. But it is important to remember that self-employment is just one component of informal employment and can therefore provide only a partial picture of the extent of informal work. Moreover, the trend in self-employment may be different from the overall trend in informal employment. When non-agricultural self-employment is declining while

[21] Each of these subregions includes only the developing countries within them, and thus not Australia, Japan or New Zealand.

Figure 8: Self-employment as percentage of non-agricultural employment, latest year available (%)

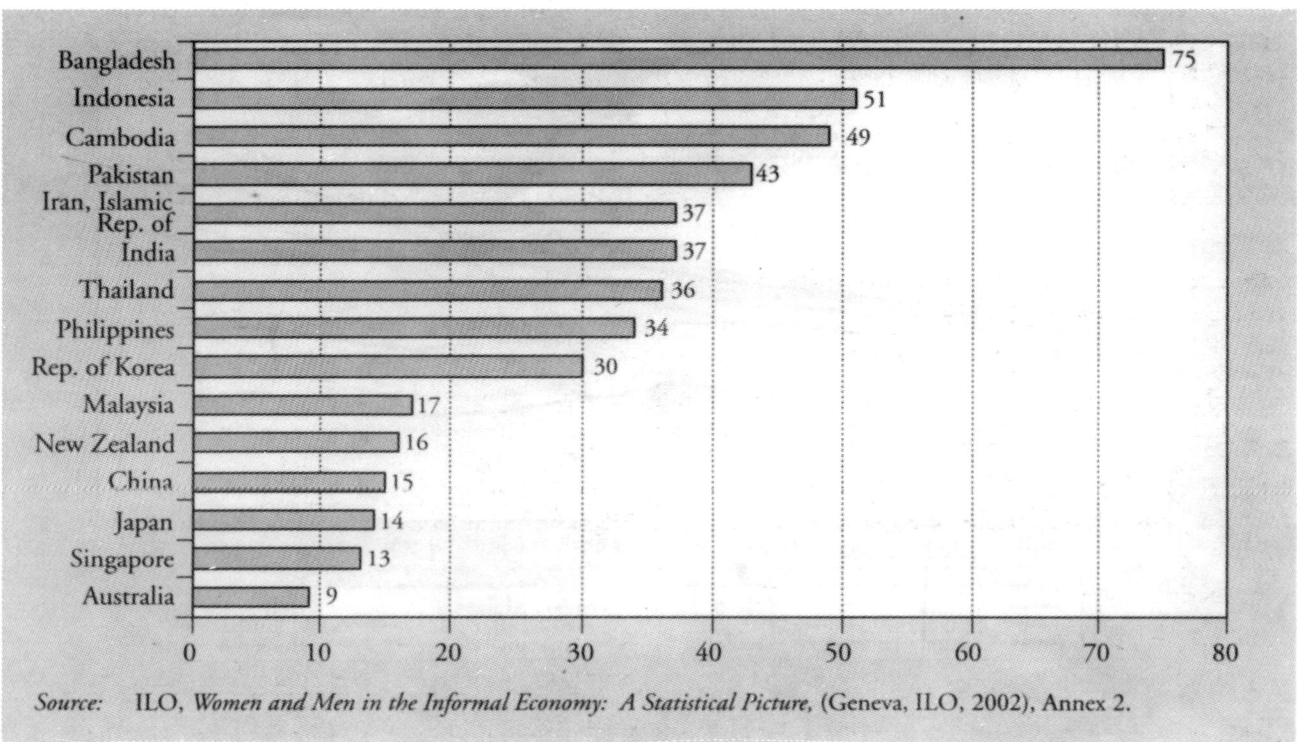

Source: ILO, *Women and Men in the Informal Economy: A Statistical Picture,* (Geneva, ILO, 2002), Annex 2.

informal wage employment is expanding even more rapidly, using non-agricultural self-employment as a proxy for informal employment would lead to an incorrect assessment of overall change. An additional consideration is that working conditions tend to be poorer in informal wage employment than in informal self-employment and therefore focusing on the latter misses worse forms of informal employment. In India, for example, the poverty rate is nearly twice as high for casual workers than for the self-employed.[22]

This caution illustrates the need for better statistics on informal employment. Without better statistics, the largest segment of the labour force in developing Asia is not adequately measured and understood. Without better statistics, it is difficult to monitor and evaluate the impact of policies on changes in the informal economy.

3.3 Wages

Rapid economic growth and large gains in productivity have led to rising real wages in some Asian developing countries that have become major exporters. Although this trend was interrupted by the financial crisis of 1997/98, there are signs that the trend is resuming.

Real manufacturing wages in China more than doubled between 1990 and 2001, reflecting exceptionally high productivity growth in the sector (Figure 9). In other open economies in East and South-East Asia such as the Republic of Korea, Malaysia and Singapore, real wages increased between 60 to 80 per cent, though the recovery was slower in Indonesia and Thailand. More modest increases of between about 10 to 20 per cent occurred in Thailand and the industrialized countries of Australia, Japan and New Zealand, whilst wages were basically flat or declining in Fiji, Mongolia, the Solomon Islands, the Philippines, India, Nepal, Pakistan and Sri Lanka.

The gender gap in manufacturing wages has narrowed in some countries, most significantly in Japan, Malaysia and the Republic of Korea – countries where the male to female wage ratio has traditionally been among the highest in the region. Despite this trend, men in these countries still earn 60 per cent more than women. In the Islamic Republic of Iran, Thailand and the Philippines, male wages are about 30 per cent higher than female wages. Wage differences in other countries are smaller or negligible.

[22] Ajit Ghose: "The employment challenge in India", in *Economic and Political Weekly*, 2004, 39(48), pp. 5106-5116.

Figure 9: Real manufacturing wage indices, selected countries, 1990-2001 (1990 = 100)

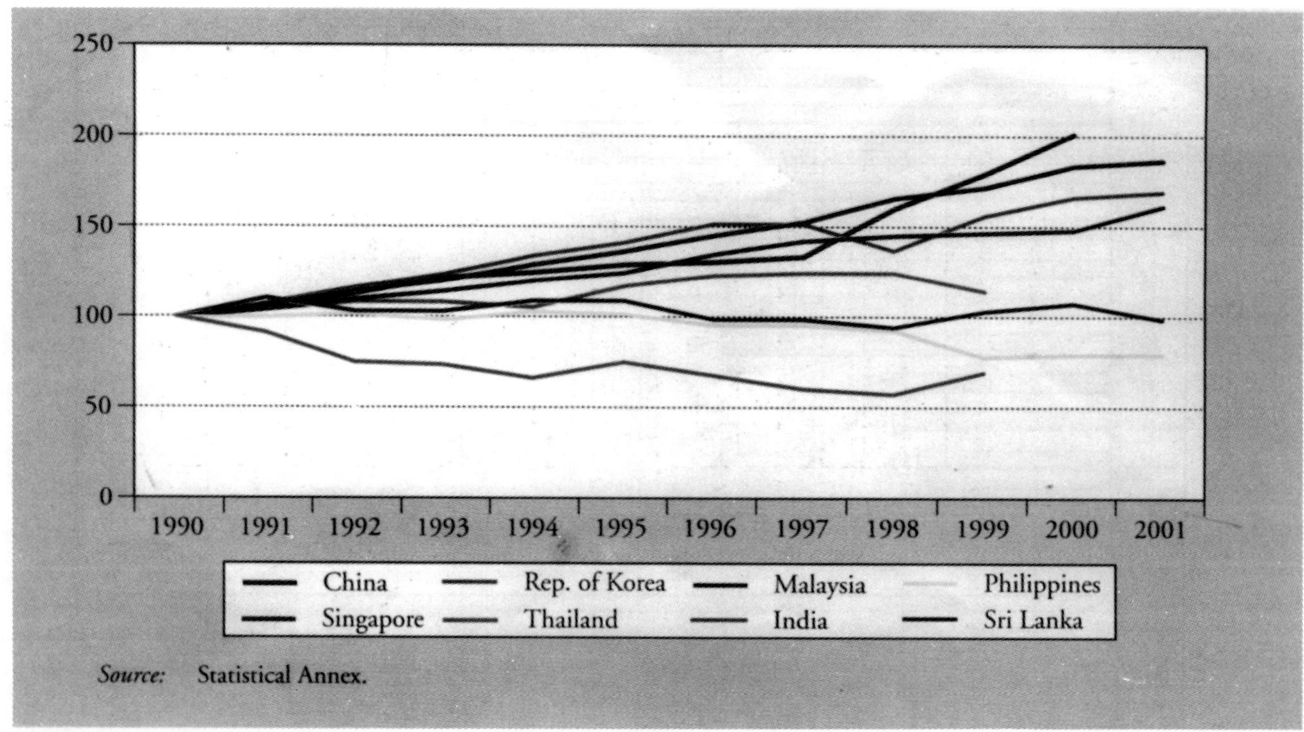

Source: Statistical Annex.

There are indications that booming economies and emerging skill shortages have pushed labour costs higher in recent years. For example, between 2001 and 2003 labour costs in China and India went up by 20 and 25 per cent, respectively (Table 5). These are large increases but their impact on the huge gap in labour costs between developing Asia and the industrialized world is negligible.

Table 5: Labour costs in selected countries

	2001(US$)	2003(US$)	Change (%)
China	0.5	0.6	20.0
India	0.8	1.0	25.0
Korea, Rep. of	8.1	9.9	22.0
Spain	10.8	13.8	28.0
United States	19.9	21.6	8.5

Source: Oxford Economic Forecasting, 2004. As reported in "Labour Cost Gap Widens between India and China", by Anil Sasi, in The *Hindu Business Line,* December 11, 2004.

3.4. Working time

Workers in developing Asia still work more hours than most of their global counterparts. While rapid economic growth and productivity gains have contributed to rising real wages in some Asian developing countries, the benefits of growth have not translated into shorter working time. In 2003, the average hours of work per week in Australia and New Zealand were less than 35 and in the Philippines and Japan between 41 and 42. Workers in other countries were spending more hours on the job: in Viet Nam 44.1 hours, in the Republic of Korea 45.9 hours, in Singapore 46.0 hours, and in India 46.7 hours per week (in 2001).

The long working time is also reflected by the large share of people working 50 hours or more a week out of the total number of employed. In the Republic of Korea, Mongolia, Cambodia, Singapore, Thailand and Pakistan more than 35 per cent of employed people work 50 hours or more per week (Figure 10). In the Philippines, Viet Nam, Bangladesh, Sri Lanka and Japan between 20 to 30 per cent of the workforce put in more than 50 hours on the job per week. But in Australia and Indonesia a smaller proportion of the employed work long hours.

The long working time in developing Asia is even more evident from the total number of annual hours worked per person. Out of the 48 economies in the world for which data is available, nine reported over 2000 annual hours worked per person (in the latest year for which data is available). The top six economies in terms of annual hours worked

Figure 10: Percentage of employed persons working 50 hours or more a week, latest year available (%)

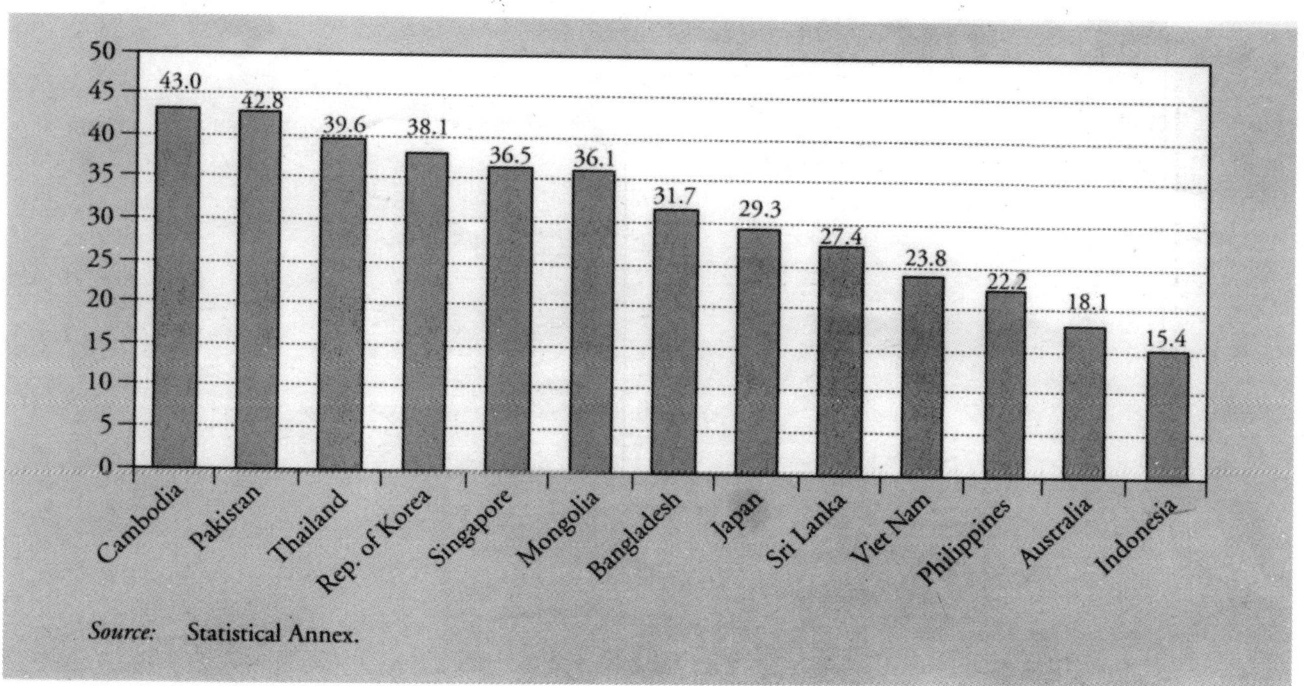

Source: Statistical Annex.

are all Asian: Thailand, Malaysia, Hong Kong (China), Sri Lanka, Bangladesh, and the Republic of Korea.[23] A Korean worker in 2001, for example, worked 34 per cent more hours annually than his or her counterpart in Honduras, Spain or the United States, 66 per cent more hours than workers in Germany and Denmark, and 79 per cent more hours than Norwegian and Dutch workers, who were at the bottom of the working time "league" (Box 2).

Trends in working time show no clear relationship with the economic performance of a country. In seven out of the eight countries for which time-series data is available, the average hours of work per week have remained stable since the mid-1990s. However, it dropped in Thailand from 51.8 hours in 1995 to 44.1 hours in 2003. The proportion of employed people working 50 hours or more per week remained unchanged in Australia, Indonesia, Japan and the Philippines, while there have been sharp declines in the Republic of Korea, Thailand and Viet Nam. Between 1995 and 2003, the share of the labour force working 50 hours or more in the Republic of Korea dropped from 47.2 to 38.1 per cent, in Thailand from 53.8 to 39.6 per cent and in Viet Nam from 50.2 to 23.8 per cent.

[23] ILO, *Key Indicators of the Labour Market*, Third Edition (Geneva, ILO, 2003), p. 239.

Box 2: Tripartite agreement on working time reduction in the Republic of Korea

The Korean Tripartite Commission formed a Special Committee for Working Hour Reduction in 2000 aimed at addressing the problem of long working hours. At the recommendation of the Special Committee, the Labour Standards Act was amended to reduce the statutory working hours from 44 hours to 40 hours per week. Other changes include new rules on overtime work such as reduced premium rates for the first four hours of overtime, while allowing overtime to be extended to 16 hours, from the previous 12 hours. The main objective of the revised Labour Standards Act is to improve the quality of work through reduced working time and the competitiveness of enterprises through greater flexibility in working time schedules. These changes are implemented gradually between 2004 and 2011, according to the type of industry and the size of business entities.

Source: Korea International Labour Foundation (KOILAF), 2005. *Current Labor Situation in Korea,* 2005 Updated Edition, pp. 15-20.

4

Social trends

4.1 Poverty

The Asia-Pacific region has made substantial progress in reducing poverty. The number of people living on less than US$1 a day dropped by about a quarter of a billion since 1990, largely due to sustained growth in China and acceleration of the economy in India, the two most populous countries in the world. Yet, the region is still home to some 689 million (more than two-thirds of the world's poor) living on less than US$1 a day. If the poverty line is raised to US$2 a day, Asia has 2 billion poor people or more than three-fourths of the world's poor.[24]

The regional figure masks diverse performances by the subregions (Table 6). The decline in income poverty has been the most remarkable in East and South-East Asia. Based on the US$1 a day poverty line, poverty has been virtually eliminated in Malaysia, Thailand and the Republic of Korea. Between 1990 and 2003, the latest date for which data is available, China, Indonesia and Viet Nam (Box 3) halved the number of those living on less than US$1 a day. These countries have already achieved the Millennium Development Goal (MDG1) of halving the US$1 poverty rate by 2015. Lao PDR and the Philippines are also close to achieving this goal.

Table 6: US$1 a day and US$2 a day poverty shares (%)

	US$1 a day total poverty		US$2 a day total poverty	
	1990	2003	1990	2003
East Asia	31.2	14.9	68.8	43.2
South-East Asia	16.6	9.3	59.3	47.8
South Asia	40.9	28.4	85.4	75.7

Source: ILO, *World Employment Report 2004-05* (Geneva, ILO, 2005).

On the other hand, the largest number of poor people lives in South Asia. Although US$1 a day poverty dropped from 40.9 per cent in 1990 to 28.4 per cent in 2003, the South Asian share is still the second highest in the world (after Sub-Saharan Africa). The poverty rate is particularly high in Nepal, Bangladesh and India. In the Pacific, although the reliability of data needs to be checked, more than 25 per cent of the population is believed to be living in poverty in Fiji, Kiribati, Micronesia, Papua New Guinea, Solomon Island, Timor-Leste and Vanuatu.

In addition to poverty among the population on a per capita basis, it is important to examine poverty among those working to earn an income. In developing Asia, as in other developing regions where no efficient social protection systems or social safety nets exist, the poor cannot afford to be unemployed and must work in order to survive and support their families. This means the problem is not so much the absence of economic activity but rather the low productive nature of that activity and low earnings. Most poor people are working (and most working very hard and long hours) but are in low productivity jobs and are not earning enough to lift themselves and their families out of poverty. If people working in poverty were able to be more productive and earn more, then poverty would decline. This is why access to decent and productive employment is essential as a sustainable route out of poverty.

[24] Asian Development Bank, *Key Indicators 2004: Poverty in Asia: Measurement, Estimates and Prospects* (Manila, ADB, 2004). Note that the data also include Central Asia.

Box 3: Growth, jobs and poverty: The success story of Viet Nam

According to World Bank data, 8 million people were lifted out of US$1 a day poverty between 1993 and 2003. In Viet Nam, 39.9 per cent of the population lived below the poverty line in 1993, but only 12 per cent did so in 2003. Urban poverty dropped from 25 to 6 per cent in this period. This was the result, among other factors, of an impressive decrease in the number of urban working poor as a consequence of more productive jobs and higher wages.

In addition, unemployment decreased considerably over the past ten years. Viet Nam's economy generated approximately 730,000 new jobs annually. This was not only a result of impressive growth rates, but also of the national programme for employment generation that supported job centres and vocational training. Over this period the private sector absorbed about 90 per cent of new entrants to the labour market.

Another contributing factor was the almost unique slowdown in population growth that started in the late 1980s and took some pressure off the labour markets by noticeably reducing the number of new entrants.

The case of Viet Nam may serve as a good example for other economies in the region but, in one respect, it also serves as a warning. Despite ten years of successful employment growth and poverty reduction in urban areas, success in rural areas has been far less impressive. Urban poverty has dropped from 66 to 36 per cent but the amount of jobs created has lagged behind labour force growth. This might turn into a burden for development. To reduce poverty further, rural areas cannot be ignored in future development strategies.

Source: ILO, *Global Employment Trends* (Geneva, ILO, 2004).

The working poor are defined as the proportion of employed persons living in a household whose members are estimated to be below the poverty line.[25] In 2004, the share of workers living on US$1 a day out of total employment was 10.9 per cent in South-East Asia, 15.7 per cent in East Asia and 35.9 per cent in South Asia (Table 7). Taking the US$2 a day poverty line, 86.7 per cent of the workers in South Asia did not earn enough to lift themselves and their families out of poverty. The corresponding figures are 58.0 per cent in South-East Asia and 46.9 per cent in East Asia.

Table 7: US$1 a day and US$2 a day working poverty shares in total employment (%)

	US$1 a day working poverty share		US$2 a day working poverty share	
	1990	2004	1990	2004
East Asia	35.9	15.7	79.1	46.9
South-East Asia	19.9	10.9	69.1	58.0
South Asia	53.0	35.9	93.1	86.7

Source: ILO, *World Employment Report 2004-05* (Geneva, ILO, 2005); and Steven Kapsos: "Estimating growth requirements for reducing poverty: Can the world halve working poverty by 2015?", Employment Strategy Papers No. 14, ILO, Geneva, 2004.

Whether measured on the basis of population or employment, poverty is predominantly a rural phenomenon for two reasons. First, even though developing Asia is becoming more and more urbanized the majority of the population is still living in rural areas where agriculture is the main source of employment. Second, the poverty rate is higher in rural areas than in urban settings. The analysis of 17 countries for which there is data shows that the ratio of rural to urban poverty rates is two times higher in Cambodia, Malaysia, Papua New Guinea, the Philippines, Thailand and Viet Nam, and is between 1.2 and 2.0 in Bangladesh, India, Lao PDR, Nepal, Pakistan, Sri Lanka and Timor-Leste. Countries where the rural rate is somewhat lower than the urban one are Fiji, Mongolia and Myanmar. Therefore, any serious effort to reduce poverty must acknowledge that there is both a geographical and a sectoral component to address.[26]

[25] ILO, *Key Indicators of the Labour Market,* Third Edition (Geneva, ILO, 2003), p. 722. Also Nomaan Majid, "The size of the working poor in developing countries", Employment Paper No. 16 (Geneva, ILO, 2001).

[26] For a detailed discussion of the policy implications, see ILO, *World Employment Report 2004-05* (Geneva, ILO, 2005), pp. 127-182.

4.2 Child labour

The Asia-Pacific region has the largest number of child workers in the 5-14 age group in the world – some 127 million, about 60 per cent of working children worldwide. In 2000, the total number of working children in the world in the 5-14 years age group was estimated at 211 million.[27] The actual number of child workers would be much higher if those children in the worst forms of child labour between 15 to 17 years of age were included. At too young an age, these children work long hours, often every day of the week, in mines, in agriculture, in construction and in brick kilns, in fisheries and car repair workshops, in homes and entertainment businesses.[28]

In 2003, the proportion of children aged 10-14 in the labour force was 5.1 per cent in East and South-East Asia and the Pacific and 13.5 per cent in South Asia (compared to a world average of 10.1 per cent). These rates are much lower than in 1990, especially in East Asia and South-East Asia and the Pacific. Countries with declines of greater than 10 percentage points are China, the Solomon Islands, Thailand and Viet Nam (Figure 11). But the changes were relatively modest in other countries. In Nepal over 40 per cent of the children aged 10-14 are still in the labour force and in Timor-Leste more than 35 per cent are working. In several other countries – Afghanistan, Bangladesh, Cambodia, Lao PDR, and the Solomon Islands – more than 20 per cent of children are in the labour force.

While the above statistics tend to underestimate the real number of child workers they do reveal an unmistakable trend: a declining proportion of children in the labour force. The uneven decline across subregions and countries mirrors the uneven reduction in poverty. Poverty and child labour are closely interlinked since poor families on the margin of survival have to weigh the cost of educating children against the value to the household of the work a child might do. The importance of the cost

[27] ILO, *Every Child Counts: New Global Estimates on Child Labour* (Geneva, ILO, 2002).

[28] For a detailed discussion, see: ILO, *Combating Child Labour in Asia and the Pacific: Progress made and challenges* (Bangkok, ILO Regional Office for Asia and the Pacific, 2005).

Figure 11: Percentage of children (aged 10-14) in the labour force, 1990 and 2003 (selected countries with 1990 data over 10%)

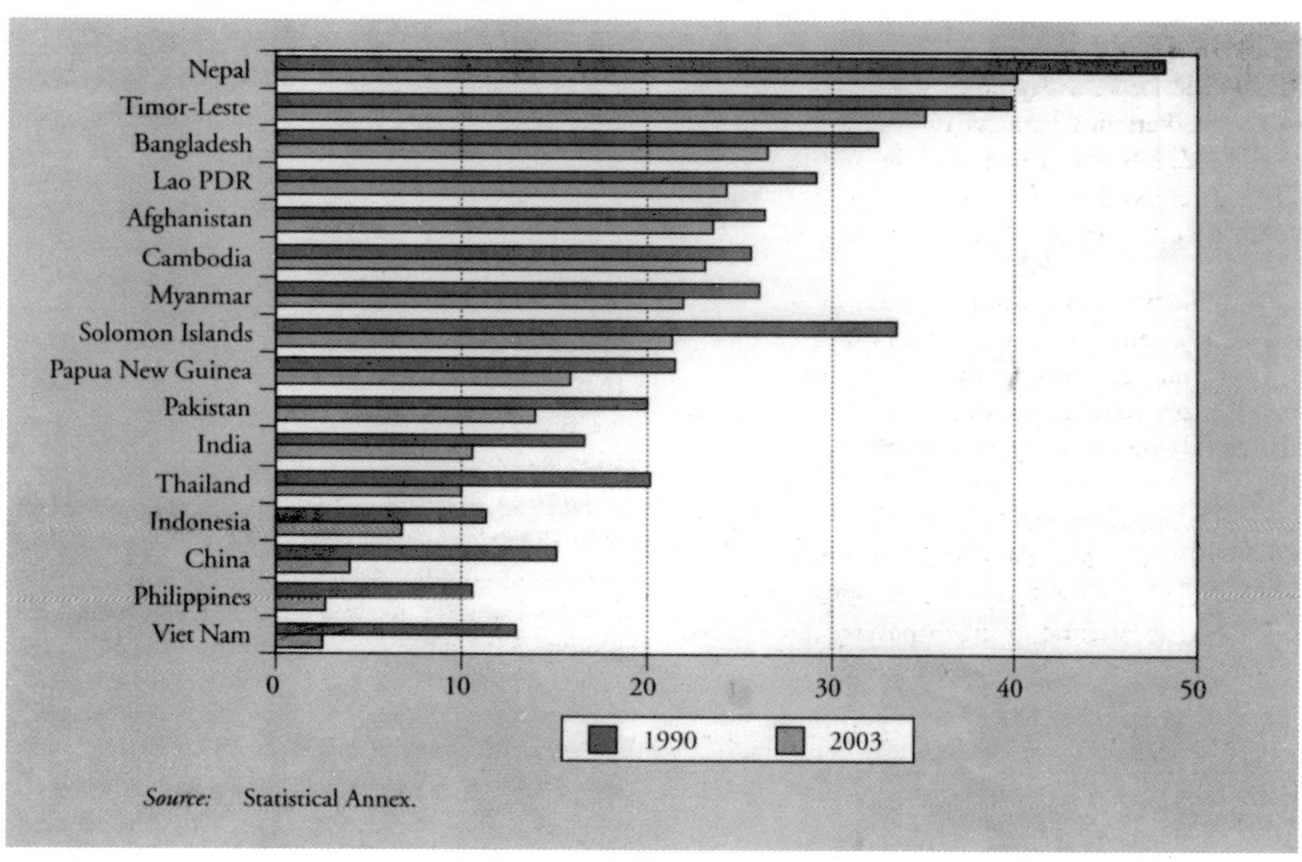

Source: Statistical Annex.

of education to poor families is clearly shown by the 2005 ILO survey on attitudes to child labour and education in Indonesia – the first of its kind in the region.[29] While parents are highly committed to the idea of educating their children, they cited the costs of education as the main factor behind why their children were out of school. In addition, where the curriculum is not matched to the needs of the local labour market, and where school facilities are not renewed and repaired for years, poor families think twice before sending their children to school. However, education looks increasingly attractive to parents when they see their children acquiring the necessary skills to obtain decent work and being able to support them in their old age.

At the same time, reducing the demand for child labour is essential. Small firms and informal sector operators hire children because they cannot afford to pay adult workers. Improving work performance and other aspects of small business operations by raising profitability helps move such enterprises from the margins of the market to a more secure position where the higher productivity of better paid adults is more useful than the low wage costs of less productive children. Equally important is the effective enforcement of child labour and education legislation, as well as the mobilization of governments, workers, employers, civil society organizations and the children and families themselves, about the risks of child labour and the importance of basic education and skills development over the long term.

Considering the hidden and often clandestine nature of child labour, including in its worst forms, child labour needs to be more adequately measured and better understood. Therefore, it is crucial that statistical data gathering and analysis be intensified in this field. SIMPOC is the statistical and monitoring unit of the ILO's International Programme on the Elimination of Child Labour and provides technical assistance to ILO member States to generate reliable, comparable and comprehensive data on child labour (Box 4).

Education data can also be an important proxy for measuring the incidence of child labour,

[29] The study was conducted by the ILO in collaboration with a leading market research company, Taylor Nelson Soffres (TNS), from January to March 2005. The survey looked at 1212 households across six provinces of Indonesia: Greater Jakarta, East Java, West Java, North Sumatra, East Kalimantan and South Sulawesi. The target group was poorer households with children of junior secondary school age, as it is these children who are most likely to become child labourers.

Box 4: Statistical Information and Monitoring Programme on Child Labour

The Statistical Information and Monitoring Programme on Child Labour (SIMPOC) was launched in 1998 in response to the growing need for more comprehensive statistics on child labour. The programme has been built on work undertaken by the ILO Bureau of Statistics from 1992 to 1997 on the development of statistical methodologies for collecting data on child labour. Over the last few years, SIMPOC has further refined the quantitative methods and survey questionnaires used in national child labour surveys and vastly extended its coverage to all major world regions. SIMPOC has also collaborated with UNICEF on the development of a new qualitative approach, the Rapid Assessment Methodology with a view to gathering information on the less visible forms of child labour, which are not easily captured by national child labour surveys. A SIMPOC External Advisory Committee was established in 2003 comprised of experts in survey methodology, data management/dissemination and child labour research (including representation from UNESCO, UNICEF, and the World Bank).

The legal and policy framework for all ILO work on child labour is provided in two fundamental ILO Conventions: The Minimum Age Convention, 1973 (No. 138) and the Worst Forms of Child Labour Convention, 1999 (No. 182). With the rapid rise in the number of ratifications of Convention No. 182, the demand for SIMPOC technical support has increased strongly. For countries that have ratified this Convention, data collection is one of the necessary first steps in fulfilling the Convention's provisions in preventing and combating the worst forms of child labour. There are six basic methods of data collection that have been applied to generate child labour statistics and information including the National Child Labour Surveys, the Rapid Assessment Methodology, Baseline Surveys, Establishment-based Surveys, Street Children Surveys and School-based Surveys. These child labour survey methodologies are not mutually exclusive and can be applied in a combined and complementary way.

since the majority of out-of-school children are working. The coordination of data collection on child labour and education is crucial in this regard.

The progressive elimination of child labour is inextricably linked to MDG2 to achieve universal primary education by 2015. Despite the progress in enrolment made throughout the 1990s, large numbers of children of primary school age are still not enrolled. In 2001, 103 million children of primary school age were not enrolled in school globally. Of these out-of-school children, 48 million were in this region, with 36 million in South Asia, the majority of who were working.[30] While the proportion of girls among out-of-school children dropped sharply – from 71 per cent in 1990 to 49 per cent in 2000 – in the East Asia and South-East Asia and Pacific subregions, the proportion of out-of-school girls in South Asia is 60 per cent or higher.[31] Girls' work constitutes a major obstacle to achieving progress in girls' education. Their work, for example, household chores, domestic services, and agricultural work is largely hidden. Often, when faced with limited resources, parents prefer to invest in the education of their sons and keep their daughter's contribution to the household economy. Efforts to increase girls' education must go hand-in-hand with efforts to progressively eliminate child labour.

4.3 Organized labour and social dialogue

Countries where workers feel their fundamental rights are respected and believe that they have a say in their treatment at work are more likely to have stable and effective labour institutions. Such institutions include trade unions and employers' organizations that provide representation for their members and a system of social dialogue offering forums for consultations and negotiations. Labour institutions have a key role in ensuring a balance between economic objectives and social goals – a major concern in the era of rapid globalization.

Unions represent a cornerstone of labour market institutions and play a vital role in promoting decent work conditions. But regardless of the workplace and the country, unions are facing the same sorts of challenges (although in some places tougher than others) relating to globalization, restructuring, privatization, and informalization. Traditional forms of action are losing their effectiveness, past gains have been renegotiated, and it is difficult for workers to make their voice heard. The ability of unions to represent and defend the interest of workers is also constrained by the shortcomings of union structures in some countries and by restrictive labour regulations and laws in others. In addition, unions in countries undergoing a transition from totalitarian regimes to democratic societies face the difficult task of adjusting to new circumstances.

Therefore, it is not surprising that the level of unionization in Asia and the Pacific is low and declining. Trade union density (membership as a proportion of the labour force)[32] in Bangladesh, Thailand, Malaysia and the Republic of Korea is around 3 to 8 per cent compared to around 10 to 12 per cent in Sri Lanka and the Philippines. Union density is the highest in developed (industrialized) economies, around 16 per cent in Japan, 17 per cent in New Zealand and over 18 per cent in Australia and Singapore (Figure 12).

Since the early 1990s, union density has declined in most Asian countries, with the exception of a few. Union density has remained stable in Bangladesh and India and increased in Singapore, especially in recent years. The main reasons behind the decline in union density are the fall in employment in previously highly organized sectors (such as manufacturing and public services), the rise

[30] UNESCO, *Education for All: The quality imperative: EFA Global Monitoring Report 2005* (Paris, UNESCO, 2004), p. 95.

[31] UNESCO, *Gender and Education For All: The Leap to Equality: EFA Global Monitoring Report 2003/4* (Paris, UNESCO, 2003), p. 50.

[32] Union density expresses union membership as a proportion of the eligible workforce. The eligibility criteria to join unions, however, shift over time and across countries, and data on the eligible workforce is not easily available. For this reason, union density is typically calculated on the basis of wage and salary earners – the group that is regarded as the main domain of the unions. Yet it is also useful to look at the number of trade union members as a percentage of the total labour force, especially because labour force data is available for more countries than for wage and salary earners. The denominator can, of course, make a very large difference in measures of trade union density, depending on the structure of employment in a country. Nonetheless, one finds that an assessment of change over time is very similar using either wage and salary earners or labour force participants as the denominator.

Figure 12: Trade union density (union membership as a proportion of labour force), by country, 1995-2002

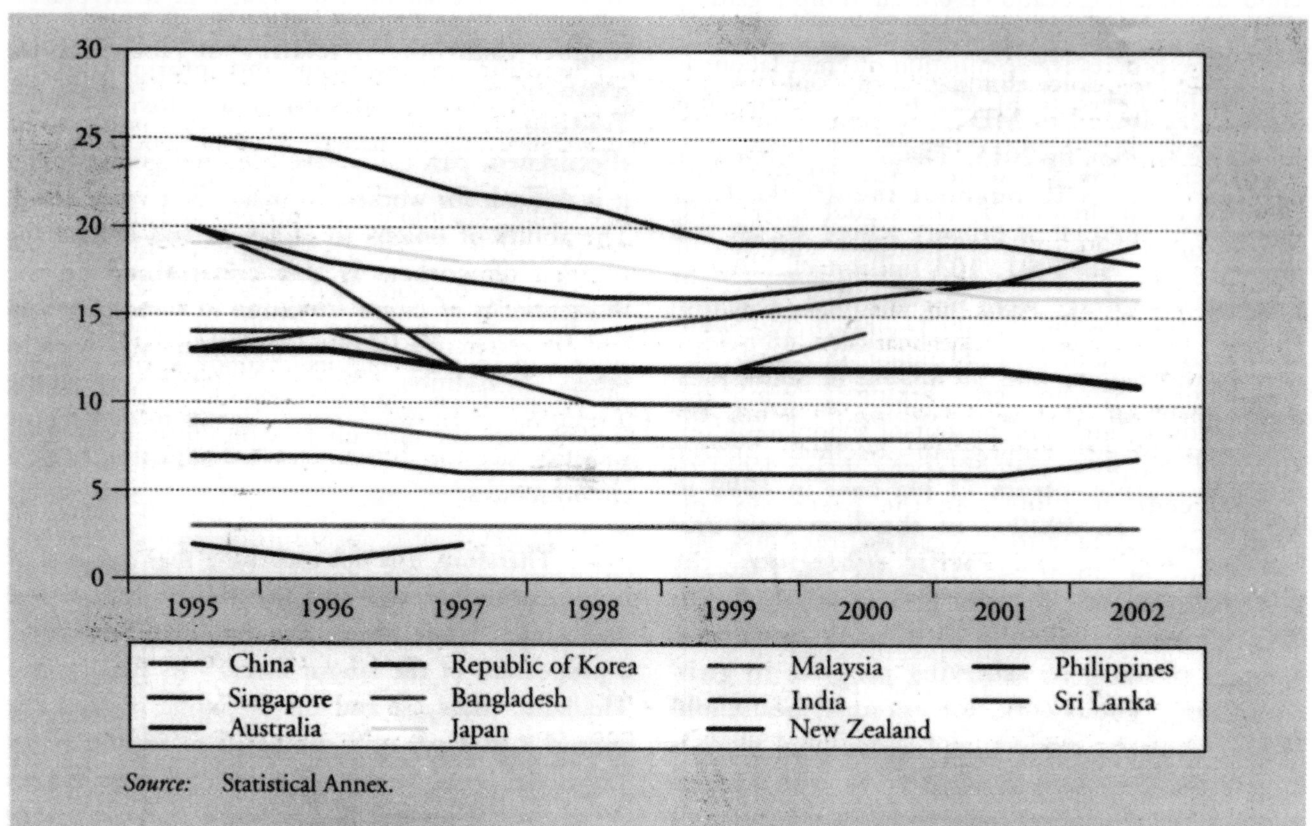

Source: Statistical Annex.

in employment in small- and medium-sized enterprises (often in the service sector), and an increase in flexible types of work contracts. Moreover, the combination of growth of foreign direct investment (FDI), rapid technological changes and increasing competition across borders have shifted the balance between capital and labour and have made traditional forms of interest representation less efficient. A pressing task facing the union movement is to address the power and influence of multinational companies.

In assessing trends in union membership, it is important to note that union influence and power cannot be measured merely in terms of the number of members. Trade union membership is an important factor in their power; but it is not the only one. This can be seen from the influence of unions in economic and social policy-making in a few economies and even more clearly in the capacity of unions in some countries to call for action, despite very low unionization rates.

Asian employers' organizations have also been experiencing formidable challenges. They have to deal with an increasing diversity of companies: the growing presence of multinational enterprises, which typically remain outside national federations, as well as the increasing diversity of national firms. Their main task is to represent the interests and provide services for this diverse business community.

Collective bargaining and social dialogue systems in Asia are very diverse, influenced by national history, regulations and economic factors. Information on collective bargaining coverage in the region is limited and dated. In 2000, collective bargaining coverage was 10 per cent in the Republic of Korea, 15 per cent in Japan, and 25 per cent in New Zealand, and an astonishing 80 per cent in Australia. However, bargaining coverage was much lower in developing Asia, ranging from 2 per cent in India to 33 per cent in the Philippines.[33]

In addition to collective bargaining, unions in many countries play a role in social dialogue. The strength of tripartite mechanisms of consultation

[33] ILO, *Organizing for Social Justice,* Report of the Director-General, International Labour Conference, 92nd Session, 2004, Table 3.5.

Box 5: The East Asian IR Net

Many industrial relations scholars and practitioners in East Asia know more about works councils in Germany than about industrial relations institutions in their neighbouring countries. In a bid to generate better knowledge in the region on national industrial relations systems the ILO has initiated the establishment of an East Asian industrial relations website, called East Asian IR Net. The website will cover ten ASEAN countries plus China, Japan and the Republic of Korea – countries with deepening economic relations through trade agreements.

With support from the Government of Japan, the East Asian IR Net will gather and present information on national frameworks for collective bargaining, social dialogue and dispute settlement. The East Asian IR Net will also establish a database on union density and collective bargaining coverage, including information on the level and topic of collective negotiations, the agenda and outcome of national tripartite dialogues, and news on major labour disputes and the way they have been resolved. Furthermore, the website will publish thematic reports on wages, productivity and other relevant issues. Once established, the East Asian IR Net could become a powerful tool for mutual learning on industrial relations in the region.

and negotiations varies across countries. In a few Asian economies, governments emphasize tripartism as a means of coordinating policies with the needs of unions and employers where the decisions of social partners can have a major impact on the competitiveness of the economy. In other countries, tripartism serves for information sharing and consultation on a variety of employment and social issues. As social dialogue provides a potentially useful mechanism for consensus building and strengthening social cohesion, information on the scope, agenda and outcome of social dialogue as well as on other aspects of national industrial relations system is needed (Box 5).

4.4 Ratification of ILO Conventions

A country's ratification of ILO Conventions provides an *indication* of its commitment to promote international labour standards. Although ratification has gone up in Asia and the Pacific in recent years the region still has the lowest average number of ratifications per country (Figure 13). Within Asia, the number of ratifications per country is highest in the industrialized economies and in some South Asian countries. Countries with the highest number of ratifications include New Zealand (59), Australia (58) and Japan (46); followed by India and Sri Lanka (each with 40); and Pakistan (34) and Bangladesh

Figure 13: Average number of ratifications of ILO Conventions per country, by region, 2005

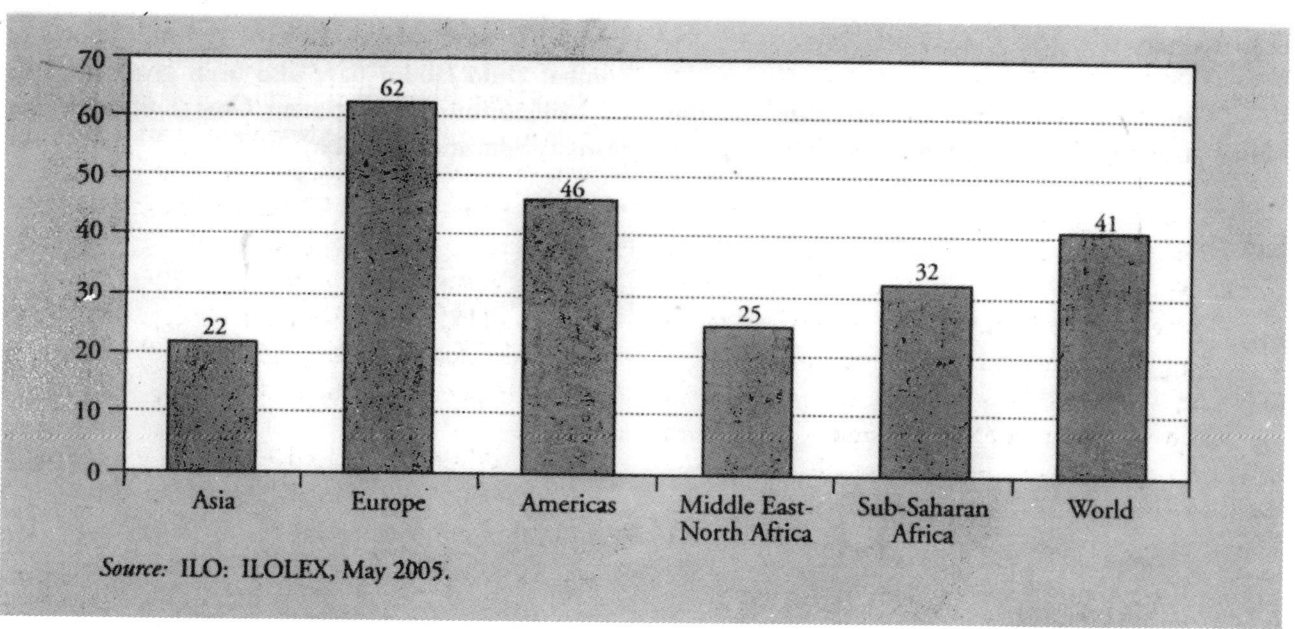

Source: ILO: ILOLEX, May 2005.

(33). Countries with only 15 or fewer ratifications are Afghanistan (15), the Solomon Islands and Thailand (14 each), Cambodia and the Islamic Republic of Iran (12 each), Nepal (9), Lao PDR (6) and Kiribati (4), and Samoa, Timor-Leste and Vanuatu (0 each). It should be noted, however, that Kiribati became an ILO member country only in 2000, Timor-Leste and Vanuatu in 2003, and Samoa in 2005.

The fundamental principles in the world of work are set out in the ILO Declaration on Fundamental Principles and Rights at Work and its related Conventions. The Declaration covers four areas: freedom of association and the right to organize and bargain collectively; the prohibition of forced labour; the abolition of child labour; and the elimination of discrimination in employment. Each of the four areas is articulated through two ILO Conventions.

Ratification by the member States of the ILO's eight fundamental Conventions has gone up. Fiji, Indonesia, Mongolia, the Philippines, Papua New Guinea and Sri Lanka have ratified all eight core Conventions. Bangladesh, Cambodia and Pakistan have ratified seven each; and Australia, Japan, Nepal and New Zealand six each. On the other hand, countries having ratified less than five fundamental Conventions are Afghanistan, China and Lao PDR (three each), Myanmar (two), the Solomon Islands (one), and Samoa, Timor-Leste and Vanuatu (zero each). It should be emphasized again, though, that these three countries became ILO member countries only recently.

Concerning the four areas of fundamental labour standards, the most worrying situation is in the field of freedom of association. As of the end of May 2005, only 13 out of 29 countries in Asia and the Pacific have ratified the Freedom of Association and Protection of the Right to Organize Convention, 1948, (No. 87) and the Right to Organize and Collective Bargaining Convention, 1949 (No. 98). Among the countries that have not ratified either of these two Conventions are some of the most populous ones in the region (China, India, the Islamic Republic of Iran, the Republic of Korea, Thailand and Viet Nam). Moreover, there are a number of active cases (17 as of end July 2005) from Asia and the Pacific pending before the Committee of Freedom of Association. This indicates that freedom of association and the right to organize and collective bargaining are still problematic in some countries.

On the positive side, the two Conventions concerning the elimination of discrimination (Equal Remuneration Convention, 1930 (No. 111) and Discrimination (Employment and Occupation) Convention, 1958 (No. 111) have the largest number of ratifications among the four areas of fundamental labour standards. The ratification and implementation of these Conventions make a valuable contribution to achieving Millennium Development Goal 3 of promoting gender equality and empowering women. In addition, recognizing the importance of giving children the proper start in life and investing in the human resources of the future, ratifications of the Minimum Age Convention, 1973 (No. 138) and particularly the Worst Forms of Child Labour Convention, 1999 (No. 182) have increased in the region. Efforts to combat child labour have also been given impetus by Millennium Development Goal 2 of achieving primary education for all by 2015.

Feature: The youth employment challenge

The youth employment challenges is given prominence in the Millennium Declaration, which resolved to "develop and implement strategies that give young people everywhere a real chance to find decent and productive work" (paragraph 20).

Young women and men aged 15 to 24 made up 20.8 per cent of Asia's labour force in 2004, but unemployed youth constituted nearly half (49.1 per cent) of the region's jobless. Within the region, South Asia has the largest unemployed youth population, almost 14.5 million in 2004. However, in the last decade it is South-East Asia that has experienced the worst relative change. Youth unemployment in this subregion more than doubled, from just under 5 million (9 per cent) in 1994 to nearly 10.5 million (17.1 per cent) in 2004. Youth unemployment rates in Indonesia and the Philippines climbed over 25 per cent – the highest rates in Asia.

The ratio of youth unemployment to adult unemployment is a good indicator of the problems that young jobseekers face compared to their adult counterparts. In South Asia in 2004 a young person was 3.7 times more likely to be unemployed than an adult, in South-East Asia 5.6 times and in East Asia 2.7 times (Table 8). This is compared to the global average where youth were 3.5 times more likely to be unemployed than adults.

In Asian developing countries for which data is available, jobless young people account for more than half of the total unemployed. One reason for this lies in the demographic profile of the countries; due to rapid population growth the proportion of youth in both the working-age population and the labour force is high. The other reason is that job creation in these countries is insufficient to absorb large number of new entrants into the labour market. In countries with higher income levels, youth unemployment is less than adult unemployment; Japan and Singapore, which have both ageing populations and low birth rates, have the lowest proportions of young people among their unemployed (Table 9).

Table 8: Youth unemployment in Asia-Pacific subregions

	Youth unemployment rate (%)		Ratios of youth to adult unemployment rates	
	1994	2004	1994	2004
East Asia	6.5	7.5	2.8	2.7
South-East Asia	9.0	17.1	4.8	5.6
South Asia	8.7	10.8	3.8	3.7

Source: ILO, *Key Indicators of the Labour Market* (4th edition) (Geneva, ILO, 2005) (forthcoming).

The ILO has estimated that halving youth unemployment would increase GDP by between 1.5 and 2.5 per cent in East Asia, between 4.6 and 7.4 per cent in South-East Asia and between 4.2 and 6.7 per cent in South Asia.[34]

Looking at the gender dimension of youth unemployment, in South-East Asia and South Asia, the unemployment rate for young women is higher

[34] ILO, *Global Employment Trends for Youth* (Geneva, ILO, 2004), Table 7, p. 21.

Table 9: Youth unemployment indicators in selected Asian countries

	Youth unemployment rate (%)	Ratio of youth to adult unemployment rates	Share of youth unemployed to total unemployed (%)
Australia (2003)	11.6	2.6	37.8
Bangladesh (2000)	10.7	11.9	79.4
Japan (2003)	10.1	2.1	19.5
Korea, Rep. of (2003)	9.6	3.6	27.5
New Zealand (2003)	10.2	2.9	39.0
Indonesia (2004)	29.6	2.8	n.a.
Pakistan (2002)	13.4	2.4	51.1
Philippines (2003)	26.3	3.5	52.5
Singapore (2003)	7.8	1.5	16.8
Sri Lanka (2003)	27.2	6.3	62.3
Thailand (2004)	4.5	4.8	48.2
Cambodia (2001)	n.a.	n.a.	59.6
Viet Nam (2004)	4.6	3.2	46.2

n.a. = not available.

Source: ILO, *Key Indicators of the Labour Market* (4th edition) (Geneva, ILO, 2005) (forthcoming), except Indonesia – Labour Force Survey 2004.

than for young men. Since the female adult unemployment rate is also higher than for males in all three subregions, it is possible that this gender differential might persist into the next generation in these two subregions. East Asia is the exception because the dominant economy, China, enjoys greater gender equality (Figure 14).

While joblessness among young people is a serious regional problem, it is only one aspect of the labour market status. A young person can be inactive (outside of the labour force), unemployed, underemployed, employed full-time, part-time or even over-employed (those who in addition to full-time employment have a secondary job). The

Figure 14: Youth unemployment rate by sex, 2004 (%)

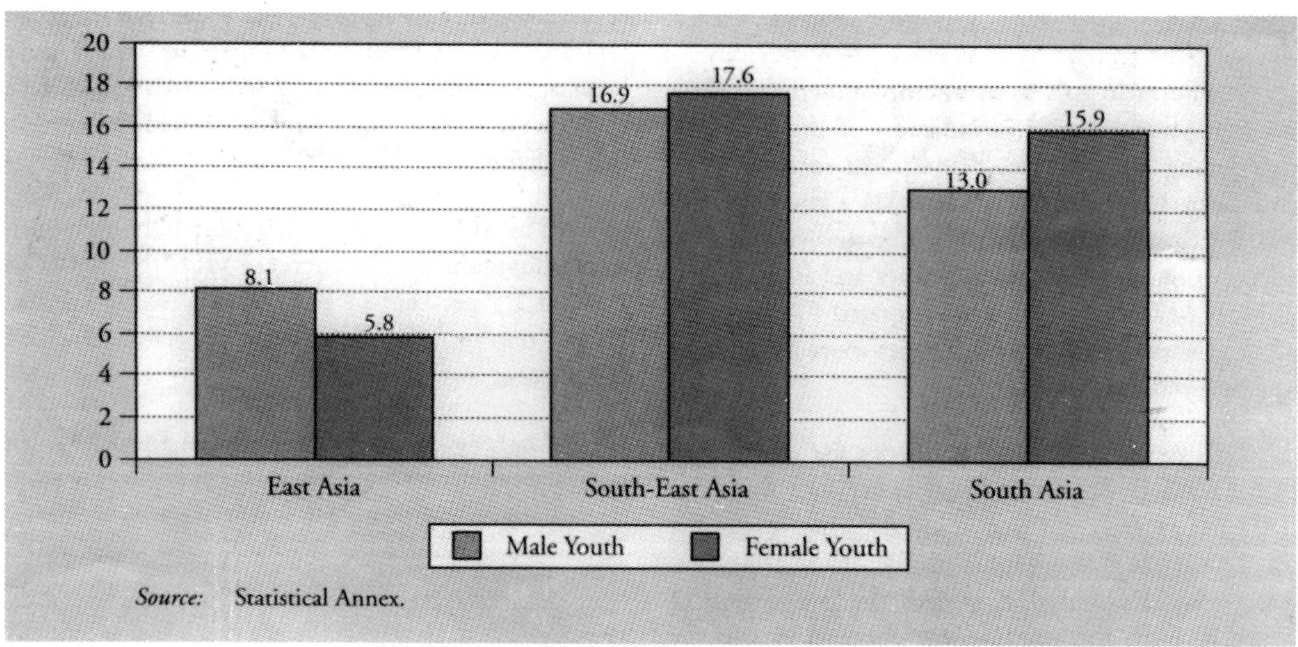

Source: Statistical Annex.

measurement of numbers and conditions in each status deserve attention as well as the "transitions" of young people from school to work (Box 6).

Concentrating on unemployment trends in countries without effective unemployment support mechanisms runs the risk of excluding from the analysis the less fortunate population who simply cannot afford to be unemployed. In several developing countries, young people from better-off families are over-represented in the unemployment numbers because it is only they who can afford to spend time looking for work and not be earning incomes. The problem, therefore, is not so much youth unemployment in developing Asia but rather the conditions of work of those who are employed.

Millions of young women and men – many of whom come from impoverished families – find themselves working long hours, without protection against hazards/risks, on short-term or informal contracts, with low pay and little or no social protection. There is a significant overlap with child labour since many of these young people above the minimum working age and below 18 years are exploited in the worst forms of child labour in the region. Indeed, there is a cruel irony in the co-existence of child labour and youth unemployment and underemployment: while there is a demand for certain types of labour that is met by children who should not be working, there is also a supply of labour from young people that goes unutilized or under-utilized.[35]

Ultimately, what young people do as the world's human resources of the present and future – as workers, entrepreneurs, innovators, change agents, citizens, leaders and tomorrow's mothers and fathers – will shape economic, social, political, and technological development. They are the world's greatest asset, but they themselves face many challenges and the international community faces the challenge of realizing fully their potentials. The international community has strongly advocated through the UN Millennium Development Goals, the development and implementation of strategies for decent and productive work for youth. A deeper understanding of the youth labour market including the development of a range of indicators and more detailed data at the country level will be needed for any strategy to be successful.

[35] IPEC, "Child labour and youth employment linkages: Conceptual framework and generic terms of reference for national policy studies and related activities", 2004, p. 6.

Box: 6: School-to-work transition surveys

The transition from childhood to adult life and especially from school to work largely determines a person's chances of escaping poverty and finding decent work. The ILO has designed a school-to-work transition survey questionnaire and assists countries in the running of the survey in order to contribute to global efforts to define the employment challenges of youth. The survey is a tool which allows countries to capture both quantitative and qualitative variables such as young people's education and training experiences, their perceptions and aspirations in terms of employment, their life goals and values, the job search process, the family's influence in the choice of occupation, barriers to and supports for entry into the labour market, the preference for wage employment or self-employment, attitudes of employers towards hiring young workers, current employment/ working conditions, control over resources, job satisfaction, marriage and family responsibilities and gender differentials. The survey focuses on transition and the variables behind the relative ease or difficulty of the transition in order to gauge where and how countries can proceed to improve the process of matching the supply and demand for youth labour.

Source: ILO, *Global Employment Trends for Youth* (Geneva, ILO, 2004).

Annex 1

Decent work indicators for Asia and the Pacific

Improving data on decent work

To promote decent work, countries need to identify decent work gaps, set targets and measure progress made in the different dimensions of decent work. Reliable statistical information is vital to achieve this. However, most countries in the region lack such information. This is mainly because the traditional focus of data collection has been on employment and unemployment, while information on rights at work, social protection, and voice and representation are very limited. The ILO has therefore launched an initiative to identify and measure a set of Decent Work Indicators (DWI).

A Task Force on Decent Work Indicators was set up in the Asia-Pacific region to assess the availability of basic information for the construction of DWI for the countries in the region; establish a regional DWI database; and provide technical advice and support to countries to develop national data compilation capacity. The DWI is neither intended nor possible to be used as cross-country comparative indices. It is a tool for each of the countries to promote decent work, as defined within their own specific economic and social contexts.

The Task Force identified an initial core set of 23 DWI that would be developed for the region, and also selected an initial list of countries for technical assistance to develop and compile DWI. The list includes: Bangladesh, China, India, Indonesia, the Islamic Republic of Iran, Pakistan, Papua New Guinea, Sri Lanka, Thailand and Viet Nam. The Task Force also suggested a second-tier of DWI that can be collected at a later stage.

The DWI is grouped under the four aspects of decent work, which are rights at work, employment, social protection and social dialogue.

List of Decent Work Indicators

Initial DWI set (1st tier)	Expanded DWI set (2nd tier)
I. Rights at work	
1. Child school non-enrolment rate 5-14 years (UNESCO data) 2. Female share of employment in ISCO 1 3. Complaints/cases brought to labour courts or ILO	1. Ratification of ILO core labour standards 2. Forced labour 3. Existence of written work contracts
II. Employment	
4. Labour force participation rate 5. Employment-population ratio 6. Informal employment 7. Number and wages of casual/daily workers (labourers) 8. Youth unemployment rate 9. Youth non-activity rate	4. Employment in informal sector 5. Place of work 6. Working poor

Initial DWI set (1st tier)	Expanded DWI set (2nd tier)
II. Employment *(continued)*	
10. Unemployment rate 11. Employment by status of employment, and branch of economic activity 12. Share of female wage employment in agriculture, industry and services sector 13. Labour productivity 14. Real per capita earnings (from national accounts)	
III. Social protection	
15. Social security coverage (for wage and salary earners) 16. Public social security expenditure (as per cent of GDP) 17. Indicator of occupational injury (fatal/non-fatal) 18. Excessive hours of work (49 hrs/w eek) 19. Low hourly pay rate	7. Occupational wages 8. Unpaid care work (from time use surveys) 9. Uninsured unemployment
IV. Social dialogue	
20. Trade union membership 21. Number of enterprises belonging to employer organization 22. Collective bargaining coverage rate 23. Strikes and lockouts	10. Membership of organizations in informal economy 11. New forms of interaction 12. Women in leadership of trade unions

In addition to information on the different aspects of decent work, it is also important to have statistics providing supplementary information on the social context of countries such as migration, poverty, income inequality, participation in micro-insurance and income support schemes, depending on the availability and relevance of the data in each country.

Each country involved in the DWI programme is preparing an inventory of data sources for DWI. This will be followed by data compilation from available statistical sources such as surveys, publications, reports, and administrative records. In addition, some countries have decided to collect parts of the data for DWI through redesigned labour force surveys.

Annex II

Statistical Annex – List of tables

Table I.1.1. Labour force – Total 1990, 1995, 1999-2003

(thousand)

	1990	1995	1999	2000	2001	2002	2003	avg. 99-03
East Asia								
China	647 245	717 553	727 910	739 920	744 320	753 600	760 750	745 300
Korea, Rep. of	18 540	20 846	21 666	22 069	22 415	22 877	22 915	22 388
Mongolia	1 011	1 181	853	848	873	902	958	887
South-East Asia								
Cambodia[b]	4 362	4 878	5 038	5 279	6 007	...	...	...
Indonesia	72 075	89 251	95 793	95 651	98 812	...	100 779	78 207
Lao PDR	1 942	2 203	...	...	...	...	...	...
Malaysia	7 042	7 893	9 151	9 616	9 699	9 886	10 240	9 719
Myanmar	20 060	22 385	23 700	24 300	24 930	25 630	...	...
Philippines	24 522	28 039	32 002	30 906	33 354	33 675	35 120	33 011
Singapore	1 516	1 748	1 976	2 193	2 120	2 129	2 150	2 114
Timor-Leste	359	389	...	...	...	...	...	...
Thailand	30 820	33 569	33 018	33 799	34 488	34 970	35 311	34 317
Viet Nam	32 809	36 709	37 700	38 400	39 490	41 200	41 900	39 738
South Asia								
Afghanistan	5 508	7 846	...	...	11 000	...	...	...
Bangladesh	46 415	53 153	...	53 512	60 300	...	...	...
India	345 996	387 308	...	...	...	...	...	...
Iran, Islamic Rep. of	16 655	19 953	...	...	...	...	...	...
Nepal[b]	7 654	8 699	9 643	...	...	...	...	...
Pakistan	29 533	31 395	36 940	38 005	41 290	42 130	43 500	40 373
Sri Lanka	6 876	6 102	6 653	6 681	6 773	7 145	7 805	7 012
Pacific Islands								
Fiji	108	...	139	153	...	...	...	...
Kiribati	...	...	...	...	...	...	...	...
Papua New Guinea	1 779	2 012	...	2 258	...	...	...	...
Solomon Islands	151	180	...	...	...	...	...	...
Vanuatu[a]	67	...	...	...	...	...	...	...
Developed (Industrialized) Economies								
Australia	8 393	8 939	9 316	9 556	9 708	9 842	9 966	9 677
Japan	63 950	66 660	67 780	67 660	67 530	66 880	66 660	67 302
New Zealand	1 606	1 779	1 878	1 892	1 926	1 979	2 015	1 938

Note: ... indicates that the data is not available. [a] indicates data for 1989 in place of 1990.
[b] indicates data for 1998 in place of 1999.

Source: KILM 3rd edition. Supplemented by ADB, *Key Indicators of Developing Asian and Pacific Countries 2004.*

Table I.1.2. Labour force – Male 1990, 1995, 1999-2003

(thousand)

	1990	1995	1999	2000	2001	2002	2003	avg. 99-03
East Asia								
China	356 230	394 427	...	...	...	...	...	...
Korea, Rep. of	11 031	12 435	12 880	13 000	13 141	13 411	13 518	13 190
Mongolia	542	629	...	...	...	...	483	...
South-East Asia								
Cambodia[b]	2 026	2 323	2 243	2 530	2 878	...	...	...
Indonesia	46 186	53 892	59 153	...	...	...	...	...
Lao PDR	1 039	1 174	...	...	...	...	...	...
Malaysia	...	...	6 064	6 275	...	...	...	...
Myanmar	11 320	12 650	...	...	...	...	...	...
Philippines	15 443	17 548	19 800	19 237	20 247	...	...	...
Singapore	933	676		1 324	...	...	...	...
Timor-Leste	198	216	...	...	...	...	...	...
Thailand	16 399	18 024	18 212	18 577	19 022	...	19 427	...
Viet Nam	16 559	18 666	...	...	...	...	...	...
South Asia								
Afghanistan	3 669	5 157	...	...	...	...	...	...
Bangladesh	27 358	31 003	...	33 452	...	...	...	...
India	240 263	266 531	...	...	...	...	...	...
Iran, Islamic Rep. of	...	...	...	...	...	...	...	...
Nepal[b]	4 609	5 217	4 833	...	...	...	...	...
Pakistan	26 263	27 388	31 480	32 003	...	...	...	...
Sri Lanka	4 323	4 069	4 440	4 430	...	...	5 245	...
Pacific Islands								
Fiji	...	...	...	...	...	...	...	...
Kiribati	...	...	...	...	...	...	...	...
Papua New Guinea	1 043	1 173	...	1 177	...	...	...	...
Solomon Islands	80	97	...	...	...	...	...	...
Vanuatu[a]	36	...	...	...	...	...	...	...
Developed (Industrialized) Economies								
Australia	4 898	5 103	5 274	5 339	5 399	5 463	5 515	5 398
Japan	38 000	39 660	40 240	40 140	39 920	39 560	39 310	39 834
New Zealand	909	990	1 029	1 036	1 050	1 079	1 093	1 057

Note: ... indicates that the data is not available. [a] indicates data for 1989 in place of 1990.
[b] indicates data for 1998 in place of 1999.

Source: KILM 3rd edition. Supplemented by ADB, *Key Indicators of Developing Asian and Pacific Countries 2004.*

Table I.1.3. Labour force – Female 1990, 1995, 1999-2003

(thousand)

	1990	1995	1999	2000	2001	2002	2003	avg. 99-03
East Asia								
China	291 014	323 125	...	...	...	...	...	...
Korea, Rep. of	7 509	8 411	8 786	9 069	9 274	9 466	9 397	9 198
Mongolia	469	550	...	...	...	...	475	...
South-East Asia								
Cambodia[b]	2 335	2 552	2 595	5 279	3 235	...	...	...
Indonesia	25 889	35 359	36 640	...	...	...	...	...
Lao PDR	903	1 029	...	...	...	...	...	...
Malaysia	...	...	3 088	3 341	...	...	...	...
Myanmar	8 738	9 733	...	...	...	...	...	...
Philippines	9 079	10 490	12 202	11 671	13 107	...	...	...
Singapore	583	676	...	868	...	...	...	...
Timor-Leste	161	173	...	...	...	...	...	...
Thailand	14 421	15 547	14 806	15 222	15 466	...	15 884	...
Viet Nam	16 250	18 044	...	...	...	...	...	...
South Asia								
Afghanistan	1 842	2 687	...	...	...	...	...	...
Bangladesh	19 056	22 151	...	20 060	...	...	...	...
India	105 733	120 780	...	...	...	...	...	...
Iran, Islamic Rep. of	...	...	...	...	...	...	...	...
Nepal[b]	3 043	3 482	4 808	...	...	...	...	...
Pakistan	3 270	4 007	5 460	6 002	...	...	...	...
Sri Lanka	2 553	765	2 213	2 251	...	...	2 560	...
Pacific Islands								
Fiji	...	...	...	...	...	...	...	...
Kiribati	...	...	...	...	...	...	...	...
Papua New Guinea	734	839	...	1 081	...	...	...	...
Solomon Islands	69	84	...	...	...	...	...	...
Vanuatu[a]	31	...	...	...	...	...	...	...
Developed (Industrialized) Economies								
Australia	3 495	3 836	4 041	4 218	4 309	4 379	4 451	4 280
Japan	25 950	27 000	27 540	27 520	27 610	27 320	27 350	27 468
New Zealand	697	788	849	856	875	899	921	880

Note: ... indicates that the data is not available. [a] indicates data for 1989 in place of 1990.
[b] indicates data for 1998 in place of 1999.

Source: KILM 3rd edition. Supplemented by ADB, *Key Indicators of Developing Asian and Pacific Countries 2004.*

Table I.2.1. Employment – Total 1990, 1995, 1999-2003

(thousand)

	1990	1995	1999	2000	2001	2002	2003	avg. 99-03
East Asia								
China**	639 090	680 650	713 940	720 850	730 250	737 400	744 320	729 352
Korea, Rep. of	18 085	20 432	20 281	21 156	21 572	22 169	22 139	21 463
Mongolia	...	768	814	809	832	871	927	850
South-East Asia								
Cambodia**	...	...	...	5 275	6 243	6 400	...	5 973
Indonesia	75 851	82 038	88 817	89 838	90 807	91 647	...	90 277
Lao PDR[a]	2 085	...	...	...	...	...	...	...
Malaysia	6 685	7 645	8 838	9 322	9 357	9 543	9 870	9 386
Myanmar**	15 221	17 590	...	...	...	...	...	...
Philippines**	22 532	25 698	27 762	27 775	30 085	30 252	31 553	29 485
Singapore	1 537	1 702	1 886	2 095	2 047	2 017	2 034	2 016
Timor-Leste[a]	385	...	...	...	...	...	...	...
Thailand	30 842	32 573	32 087	33 001	33 484	34 263	34 677	33 502
Viet Nam	...	...	38 120	38 368	39 094	40 162	41 179	39 385
South Asia								
Afghanistan	5 981	...	...	...	...	...	...	...
Bangladesh	50 159	...	...	51 764	...	...	...	51 764
India[b]	311 949	350 309	...	374 638	373 325	389 645	...	379 203
Iran, Islamic Rep. of[a]	12 108	14 542	...	...	...	...	...	...
Nepal	...	...	9 463	...	...	...	...	9 463
Pakistan**	29 797	31 407	37 296	36 847	37 481	38 882	39 900	38 081
Sri Lanka	5 964	5 316	6 159	6 308	6 212	6 663	6 943	6 457
Pacific Islands								
Fiji[a,**]	89	97	114	112	...	...	...	113
Kiribati[a]	11	8	...	...	...	...	...	...
Papua New Guinea[a]	1 879	...	...	...	...	...	...	...
Solomon Islands[a]	26	33	...	...	...	...	...	...
Vanuatu	...	...	...	...	...	...	...	...
Developed (Industrialized) Economies								
Australia	7 837	8 218	8 720	8 951	9 063	9 248	9 459	9 088
Japan	62 490	64 570	64 620	64 460	64 120	63 300	63 160	63 932
New Zealand	1 481	1 633	1 750	1 779	1 823	1 877	1 921	1 830

Notes: Iran, Islamic Rep. of: 1991: Asian Productivity Organization (APO), Population census; 1996: ESCAP; Others years: APO, Official estimates. Singapore: Labour force surveys except 2000: Population census. Sri Lanka: Geographical coverage: Excluding northern and eastern province, 1990, 2003: whole country.

... indicates that the data is not available.

Source: ILO, Laborsta-on-line (Table 2), [a] ILO 2003-2004 Key Indicators of the Labour Market (Table 2). 21 January 2005. [b] Data from indialabourstat website. See details of sources and calculations, ** latest year data from ADB, *Key Indicators of Developing Asian and Pacific Countries.*

Table I.2.2. Employment – Male 1990, 1995, 1999-2003

(thousand)

	1990	1995	1999	2000	2001	2002	2003	avg. 99-03
East Asia								
China	...	...	...	...	...	...	...	...
Korea, Rep. of	10 709	12 176	11 978	12 387	12 581	12 944	13 031	12 584
Mongolia	...	407	427	417	425	440	469	436
South-East Asia								
Cambodia	...	...	...	2 538	3 017	...	...	2 778
Indonesia	46 428	51 686	54 908	...	...	58 583	...	56 746
Lao PDR	1 110	...	...	...	...	...	...	...
Malaysia	4 311	5 057	5 851	6 086	6 056	6 142	6 324	6 092
Myanmar	...	...	...	...	...	...	...	...
Philippines	14 347	16 193	17 131	17 258	18 334	...	...	17 574
Singapore	917	1 044	1 087	1 271	1 149	1 137	1 123	1 153
Timor-Leste	...	...	...	...	...	...	...	...
Thailand	16 456	17 778	17 721	18 165	18 471	18 872	19 082	18 462
Viet Nam	...	...	19 029	19 292	19 743	20 356	20 959	19 876
South Asia								
Afghanistan	3 946	...	...	...	...	...	...	...
Bangladesh	30 443	...	...	32 369	...	...	...	32 369
India	228 940	256 504	...	267 261	278 818	285 848	...	277 309
Iran, Islamic Rep. of	...	...	...	...	...	...	...	...
Nepal	...	...	4 736	...	...	...	...	4 736
Pakistan	26 324	27 591	32 099	31 688	32 233	33 189	...	32 302
Sri Lanka	3 977	3 661	...	4 256	4 278	4 432	4 746	4 428
Pacific Islands								
Fiji	...	...	...	...	...	...	...	...
Kiribati	...	...	...	...	...	...	...	...
Papua New Guinea	1 105	...	...	...	...	...	...	...
Solomon Islands	...	...	...	...	...	...	...	...
Vanuatu	...	...	...	...	...	...	...	...
Developed (Industrialized) Economies								
Australia	4 583	4 677	4 918	5 006	5 035	5 135	5 227	5 064
Japan	37 130	38 430	38 310	38 180	37 830	37 360	37 190	37 774
New Zealand	835	913	957	973	994	1 025	1 045	999

Notes: Iran, Islamic Rep. of 1991: Asian Productivity Organization (APO), Population census; 1996: ESCAP; Others years: APO, Official estimates. Singapore: Labour force surveys except 2000; Population census. Sri Lanka: Geographical coverage: Excluding northern and eastern province, 1990, 2003: whole country.

... indicates that the data is not available.

Source: ILO, Laborsta-on-line (Table 2), [a] ILO 2003-2004 Key Indicators of the Labour Market (Table 2). 21 January 2005. [b] Data from indialabourstat website. See details of sources and calculations, ** latest year data from ADB, *Key Indicators of Developing Asian and Pacific Countries.*

Table I.2.3. Employment – Female 1990, 1995, 1999-2003

(thousand)

	1990	1995	1999	2000	2001	2002	2003	avg. 99-03
East Asia								
China	...	...	...	...	...	...	...	...
Korea, Rep. of	7 376	8 256	8 303	8 769	8 991	9 225	9 108	8 879
Mongolia	...	361	387	392	408	431	458	415
South-East Asia								
Cambodia	...	...	...	2 737	3 226	...	...	2 982
Indonesia	29 423	31 729	33 908	...	...	33 064	...	33 486
Lao PDR	975	...	...	...	...	...	...	...
Malaysia	2 374	2 588	2 987	3 236	3 301	3 401	3 546	3 294
Myanmar	...	...	...	...	...	...	...	...
Philippines	8 185	9 505	10 631	10 516	11 751	...	...	10 966
Singapore	620	658	799	824	898	880	911	862
Timor-Leste	172	...	...	...	...	...	...	...
Thailand	14 386	14 795	14 366	14 836	15 013	15 391	15 596	15 040
Viet Nam	...	...	19 091	19 076	19 257	19 807	20 217	19 490
South Asia								
Afghanistan	2 035	...	...	...	...	...	...	...
Bangladesh	19 716	...	...	19 395	...	...	...	19 395
India	83 009	93 805	...	107 377	94 507	103 797	...	101 894
Iran, Islamic Rep. of	...	...	...	...	...	...	...	...
Nepal	...	...	4 727	...	...	...	...	4 727
Pakistan	3 473	3 816	5 197	5 159	5 248	5 693	...	5 324
Sri Lanka	1 987	1 655	...	2 052	1 934	2 231	2 197	2 104
Pacific Islands								
Fiji	...	...	...	...	...	...	...	...
Kiribati	...	...	...	...	...	...	...	...
Papua New Guinea	774	...	...	...	...	...	...	...
Solomon Islands	...	...	...	...	...	...	...	...
Vanuatu	...	...	...	...	...	...	...	...
Developed (Industrialized) Economies								
Australia	3 253	3 541	3 803	3 945	4 028	4 113	4 232	4 024
Japan	25 360	26 140	26 320	26 300	26 290	25 940	25 970	26 164
New Zealand	646	720	794	806	830	852	876	831

Notes: Iran, Islamic Rep. of: 1991: Asian Productivity Organization (APO), Population census; 1996: ESCAP; Others years: APO, Official estimates. Singapore: Labour force surveys except 2000: Population census. Sri Lanka: Geographical coverage: Excluding northern and eastern province, 1990, 2003: whole country,
... indicates that the data is not available

Source: ILO, Laborsta-on-line (Table 2), [a] ILO 2003-2004 Key Indicators of the Labour Market (Table 2). 21 January 2005. [b] Data from indialabourstat website. See details of sources and calculations, ** latest year data from ADB, *Key Indicators of Developing Asian and Pacific Countries.*

Table II.1.1. Labour Force Participation Rate (aged 15-64) 1990, 1995, 2000, 2010

(per cent)

	Total				Male				Female			
	1990	1995	2000	2010	1990	1995	2000	2010	1990	1995	2000	2010
East Asia												
China	84.9	85.4	84.9	82.6	89.6	90.0	89.5	87.3	79.9	80.3	80.0	77.6
Korea, Rep. of	64.4	67.1	68.9	72.3	77.4	79.2	79.8	80.1	51.1	54.7	57.8	64.2
Mongolia	81.6	81.5	81.7	82.4	87.5	86.8	86.3	85.9	75.6	76.4	77.1	78.9
South-East Asia												
Cambodia	85.6	87.1	84.0	84.3	86.3	88.4	84.2	84.8	85.2	85.9	83.9	83.9
Indonesia	68.3	69.6	71.2	74.5	84.4	84.3	84.5	85.2	52.1	54.8	57.8	63.7
Lao PDR	83.9	84.2	83.9	83.8	91.2	91.1	90.3	89.4	76.9	77.6	77.7	78.3
Malaysia	65.4	66.2	66.5	67.5	84.0	83.2	82.0	80.1	46.4	48.7	50.7	54.7
Myanmar	79.3	79.0	78.9	78.5	90.1	89.7	89.5	88.8	68.5	68.4	68.4	68.5
Philippines	65.7	66.3	66.9	68.5	83.0	82.8	82.6	82.6	48.1	49.5	51.1	54.2
Singapore	69.2	70.1	69.7	65.1	83.8	84.9	83.6	77.3	54.4	55.3	55.3	52.5
Timor-Leste	84.0	84.3	82.3	82.2	89.8	90.1	85.8	88.0	77.8	79.2	76.3	75.6
Thailand	84.0	83.9	83.8	83.2	89.5	89.6	89.7	89.6	78.5	78.2	78.0	76.9
Viet Nam	84.5	82.9	81.4	78.1	88.1	86.2	84.5	81.1	81.0	79.6	78.3	75.1
South Asia												
Afghanistan	68.7	68.6	68.5	68.5	87.9	87.1	86.3	84.9	48.1	48.7	49.5	50.9
Bangladesh	78.8	78.9	78.8	78.9	89.4	89.1	88.7	88.2	67.3	67.8	68.2	69.0
India	66.0	66.4	66.5	67.0	87.9	87.6	86.9	85.9	42.4	43.5	44.6	46.6
Iran, Islamic Rep. of	53.9	55.1	55.6	62.0	83.1	82.3	79.9	80.7	22.2	26.3	30.0	42.6
Nepal	73.7	73.3	73.0	72.3	89.1	88.1	87.1	85.2	57.4	57.7	58.2	59.0
Pakistan	60.4	60.9	62.1	65.1	87.9	86.9	85.9	84.7	29.5	33.2	36.9	44.8
Sri Lanka	64.2	64.8	65.1	67.0	83.7	83.2	82.5	82.6	42.8	44.7	46.5	50.7
Pacific Islands												
Fiji	57.0	59.2	61.8	66.9	87.9	85.3	84.4	81.9	28.1	32.8	39.0	51.1
Kiribati	...	...	...	...	...	...	...	...	...	...	...	...
Papua New Guinea	79.2	79.2	78.6	78.1	89.2	88.5	87.3	86.1	68.6	69.3	69.1	69.4
Solomon Islands	87.2	87.3	85.6	84.4	91.6	91.0	86.9	88.9	83.8	82.5	81.9	79.8
Vanuatu	...	...	...	...	...	...	...	...	...	...	...	...
Developed (Industrialized) Economies												
Australia	73.5	74.7	75.1	74.4	84.7	84.4	83.2	80.2	61.9	64.8	66.9	68.4
Japan	70.2	71.9	73.3	75.3	84.2	84.5	85.0	84.6	56.2	59.2	61.6	66.0
New Zealand	72.5	74.3	75.2	74.3	82.7	83.2	82.4	79.4	62.6	65.6	67.8	69.3

Source: Calculated ILO database, Estimates and Projections of the Economically Active Population, 1950-2010.

Table II.2.1. Employment-to-population ratio – Total 1990, 1995, 1999-2003

(per cent)

	1990	1995	1999	2000	2001	2002	2003	avg. 99-03
East Asia								
China	77.9	76.8	76.8	76.6	76.4	76.0	...	76.4
Korea, Rep. of	56.9	59.1	55.7	57.4	58.0	59.0	58.4	57.7
Mongolia	...	55.3	52.8	51.2	51.4	52.5	54.5	52.5
South-East Asia								
Cambodia	...	...	...	63.6	70.4	...	...	83.9
Indonesia	66.5	63.8	63.4	62.7	62.3	61.7	...	62.5
Lao PDR	89.8	...	...	...	...	...	...	...
Malaysia	57.8	57.9	59.3	60.7	59.5	59.2	59.8	59.7
Myanmar	59.8	...	...	...	...	...	...	...
Philippines	62.4	62.1	59.6	57.9	61.1	...	...	59.5
Singapore	64.2	62.1	61.7	66.7	63.7	61.3	60.3	62.7
Timor-Leste	88.9	...	...	...	...	...	...	...
Thailand	81.4	77.9	71.0	71.5	71.8	72.6	72.6	71.9
Viet Nam	...	...	74.6	73.2	72.8	73.1	73.2	73.4
South Asia								
Afghanistan	60.3	...	...	...	...	...	...	...
Bangladesh	78.7	...	...	63.5	...	...	...	63.5
India	57.7	58.1	...	55.4	54.1	55.4	...	55.0
Iran, Islamic Rep. of	39.7	43.4	...	...	...	...	...	...
Nepal	...	...	71.4	...	...	...	...	71.4
Pakistan	47.6	44.7	47.6	45.8	45.0	45.2	...	45.9
Sri Lanka	54.0	43.7	46.3	46.4	44.9	47.4	48.6	46.7
Pacific Islands								
Fiji	19.5	19.7	21.3	...	...	...	...	21.3
Kiribati	...	...	...	...	...	...	...	...
Papua New Guinea	81.2	...	...	...	...	...	...	...
Solomon Islands	...	16.6	...	...	...	...	...	...
Vanuatu	...	...	...	...	...	...	...	...
Developed (Industrialized) Economies								
Australia	58.8	58.0	58.0	58.7	58.7	59.1	59.7	58.9
Japan	62.0	61.2	60.0	59.5	59.1	58.2	58.0	58.9
New Zealand	56.1	57.8	59.2	59.5	60.2	61.2	61.8	60.4

Source: Employment: Laborsta, KILM, Population 15+: World Bank, *World Development Indicators.* 31 January 2005.

Table II.2.2. Employment-to-population ratio – Male 1990, 1995, 1999-2003

	1990	1995	1999	2000	2001	2002	2003	avg. 99-03
East Asia								
China	...	...	...	...	...	...	...	...
Korea, Rep. of	67.7	70.8	66.3	67.7	68.1	69.4	69.2	68.1
Mongolia	...	59.2	56.4	53.8	53.4	54.0	56.1	54.7
South-East Asia								
Cambodia	...	...	...	64.7	71.1	...	...	85.7
Indonesia	81.7	80.7	79.1	...	...	79.7	...	79.4
Lao PDR	97.8	...	...	...	...	...	...	...
Malaysia	74.0	76.1	78.1	78.8	76.6	75.9	76.3	77.1
Myanmar	...	...	...	...	...	...	...	...
Philippines	79.6	78.4	73.6	72.0	74.4	...	...	73.4
Singapore	76.8	76.3	69.9	79.1	69.8	67.5	65.1	70.3
Timor-Leste	...	...	...	...	...	...	...	...
Thailand	88.2	86.4	80.5	81.0	81.5	82.3	82.2	81.5
Viet Nam	...	...	76.7	76.0	75.8	76.2	76.5	76.2
South Asia								
Afghanistan	76.9	...	...	...	...	...	...	...
Bangladesh	91.8	...	...	79.4	...	...	...	79.4
India	82.1	82.5	...	76.7	78.4	78.7	...	78.0
Iran, Islamic Rep. of	...	...	...	...	...	...	...	...
Nepal	...	...	70.1	...	...	...	...	70.1
Pakistan	79.5	76.3	78.4	75.0	73.9	73.8	...	75.3
Sri Lanka	68.6	57.9	...	63.0	62.4	63.7	67.2	64.1
Pacific Islands								
Fiji	...	...	...	...	...	...	...	...
Kiribati	...	...	...	...	...	...	...	...
Papua New Guinea	91.5	...	...	...	...	...	...	...
Solomon Islands	...	...	...	...	...	...	...	...
Vanuatu	...	...	...	...	...	...	...	...
Developed (Industrialized) Economies								
Australia	69.4	66.8	66.1	66.3	65.8	66.3	66.6	66.2
Japan	75.8	75.0	73.3	72.7	71.9	70.9	70.4	71.8
New Zealand	64.8	66.5	67.0	67.5	68.0	69.2	69.5	68.2

Source: Employment: Laborsta, KILM, Population 15+: World Bank, *World Development Indicators*. 31 January 2005.

Table II.2.3. Employment-to-population ratio – Female 1990, 1995, 1999-2003

	1990	1995	1999	2000	2001	2002	2003	avg. 99-03
East Asia								
China	...	...	...	...	...	...	...	...
Korea, Rep. of	46.1	47.5	45.3	47.2	48.0	48.8	47.7	47.4
Mongolia	...	51.5	49.3	48.6	49.4	51.0	53.0	50.3
South East Asia								
Cambodia	...	...	...	62.6	69.7	...	...	82.3
Indonesia	51.4	49.2	47.9	...	...	44.1	...	46.0
Lao PDR	82.1	...	...	...	...	...	...	...
Malaysia	41.4	39.5	40.3	42.4	42.2	42.4	43.2	42.1
Myanmar	...	...	...	...	...	...	...	...
Philippines	45.3	45.9	45.6	43.8	47.7	...	...	45.7
Singapore	51.7	48.0	53.3	53.8	57.2	54.7	55.3	54.9
Timor-Leste	81.5	...	...	...	...	...	...	...
Thailand	74.9	69.6	62.0	62.6	62.6	63.4	63.5	62.8
Viet Nam	...	...	72.7	70.5	69.6	70.1	70.0	70.6
South Asia								
Afghanistan	42.4	...	...	...	...	...	...	...
Bangladesh	64.6	...	...	47.6	...	...	...	47.6
India	31.7	32.1	...	32.8	28.3	30.5	...	30.5
Iran, Islamic Rep. of	...	...	...	...	...	...	...	...
Nepal	...	...	72.8	...	...	...	...	72.8
Pakistan	11.8	11.2	13.9	13.5	13.2	13.9	...	13.6
Sri Lanka	38.0	28.4	...	30.0	27.7	31.5	30.4	29.9
Pacific Islands								
Fiji	...	...	...	...	...	...	...	...
Kiribati	...	...	...	...	...	...	...	...
Papua New Guinea	69.9	...	...	...	...	...	...	...
Solomon Islands	...	...	...	...	...	...	...	...
Vanuatu	...	...	...	...	...	...	...	...
Developed (Industrialized) Economies								
Australia	48.4	49.3	50.1	51.3	51.7	52.1	53.0	51.6
Japan	49.0	48.3	47.4	47.1	47.0	46.3	46.3	46.8
New Zealand	47.8	49.6	51.9	52.1	52.9	53.7	54.5	53.0

Source: Employment: Laborsta, KILM, Population 15+: World Bank, *World Development Indicators.* 31 January 2005.

Table II.3.1. Unemployment – Total 1990, 1995, 1999-2003

(per cent of total labour force)

	1990	1995	1999	2000	2001	2002	2003	avg. 99-03
East Asia								
China	2.5	2.9	3.1	3.1	3.6	4.0	4.3	3.6
Korea, Rep. of	2.4	2.0	6.3	4.1	3.8	3.1	3.4	4.1
Mongolia	...	5.5	4.7	4.6	4.6	3.4	3.5	4.2
South-East Asia								
Cambodia	...	...	...	2.5	2.8	3.0	3.5	3.0
Indonesia	...	...	6.4	6.1	8.1	8.9	9.1	7.7
Lao PDR	...	...	...	...	...	...	...	...
Malaysia	5.1	3.1	3.4	3.0	3.5	3.5	3.6	3.4
Myanmar	...	...	...	...	...	...	...	...
Philippines	8.1	8.4	9.6	10.1	9.8	11.4	[illegible].4	10.5
Singapore	1.7	2.7	4.6	4.4	3.4	5.2	5.4	4.6
Timor-Leste	...	...	...	...	...	...	...	...
Thailand	2.2	1.1	3.0	2.4	2.6	1.8	1.5	2.3
Viet Nam	...	...	...	6.4	6.3	6.0	5.8	6.1
South Asia								
Afghanistan	...	...	...	...	3.4	3.4	3.3	...
Bangladesh	1.9	2.6	...	3.3	...	...	...	...
India[a]	...	2.2	...	4.3	...	...	...	...
Iran, Islamic Rep. of	...	...	...	12.6	12.4	12.3	...	...
Nepal	...	...	1.1	...	...	...	...	...
Pakistan	3.1	5.4	5.9	7.8	7.8	8.3	8.3	7.6
Sri Lanka	14.4	12.5	9.1	8.0	7.7	8.7	9.2	8.5
Pacific Islands								
Fiji	6.4	5.4	...	...	...	...	...	...
Kiribati	...	...	1.5	...	...	...	...	...
Papua New Guinea	...	...	...	2.8	...	...	...	...
Solomon Islands	...	...	...	...	4.9	...	...	...
Vanuatu	...	...	...	...	...	...	...	...
Developed (Industrialized) Economies								
Australia	6.9	8.4	7.0	6.4	6.9	6.4	6.0	6.5
Japan	2.1	3.2	4.7	4.7	5.0	5.4	5.3	5.0
New Zealand	7.8	6.3	6.8	6.0	5.3	5.2	4.7	5.6

Note: Australia: 1995: estimates based on population census; Bangladesh: 1995 column shows data for 1996: persons aged 10 and over; Korea, Rep. of: 1992, 2000: population census: Pakistan: 1990: computed from 87-88 survey results; Singapore: 1990, 2000: population census, Sri Lanka: 1990, 2003: whole country Laborsta data has been supplemented by data on unemployment rate from ADB, *Asian Development Outlook 2005* (Table A6).

Source: Laborsta-on-line (Table 3A), [a] ILO 2003-2004 Key Indicators of the Labour Market (Table 8A). 31 January 2005.

Table II.3.2. Unemployment – Male 1990, 1995, 1999-2003

(per cent of total labour force)

	1990	1995	1999	2000	2001	2002	2003	avg. 99-03
East Asia								
China	...	...	...	...	...	...	...	...
Korea, Rep. of	2.9	2.3	7.1	4.7	4.3	3.5	3.6	4.6
Mongolia	...	5.0	4.1	4.1	4.2	3.5	3.2	3.8
South-East Asia								
Cambodia	...	...	...	2.1	1.5	...	...	1.8
Indonesia	...	...	...	...	...	...	...	...
Lao PDR	...	...	...	...	...	...	...	...
Malaysia	...	2.8	3.5	3.0	3.4	3.3	3.6	3.4
Myanmar	...	...	...	...	...	...	...	...
Philippines	7.1	7.7	9.7	10.3	9.4	...	...	9.8
Singapore	1.9	2.7	4.5	4.0	3.5	5.4	5.5	4.6
Timor-Leste	...	...	...	...	...	...	...	...
Thailand	2.1	0.9	3.0	2.4	2.7	2.0	1.6	2.3
Viet Nam	...	...	...	...	2.3	...	...	2.3
South Asia								
Afghanistan	...	...	...	...	...	...	...	...
Bangladesh	2.0	...	...	3.2	...	...	...	3.2
India[a]	...	2.4	...	4.3	...	...	...	4.3
Iran, Islamic Rep. of	...	...	...	8.1	8.4	8.2	...	8.2
Nepal	...	...	1.5	...	...	...	...	1.5
Pakistan	3.4	4.1	4.2	6.1	6.1	6.7	...	5.8
Sri Lanka	9.1	8.8	7.4	6.4	5.8	6.5	6.4	6.5
Pacific Islands								
Fiji	...	...	...	...	...	...	...	...
Kiribati	...	...	...	...	...	...	...	...
Papua New Guinea	9.0	...	...	4.3	...	...	...	4.3
Solomon Islands	...	...	...	...	...	...	...	...
Vanuatu	...	...	...	...	...	...	...	...
Developed (Industrialized) Economies								
Australia	6.7	8.7	7.2	6.5	7.1	6.6	5.9	6.7
Japan	2.0	3.1	4.8	4.9	5.2	5.5	5.5	5.2
New Zealand	8.2	6.2	7.0	6.1	5.4	5.1	4.4	5.6

Note: Australia: 1995: estimates based on population census; Bangladesh: 1995 column shows data for 1996: persons aged 10 and over; Korea, Rep. of: 1992, 2000: population census: Pakistan: 1990: computed from 87-88 survey results; Singapore: 1990, 2000: population census, Sri Lanka: 1990, 2003: whole country Laborsta data has been supplemented by data on unemployment rate from ADB, *Asian Development Outlook 2005* (Table A6).

Source: Laborsta-on-line (Table 3A), [a]ILO 2003-2004 Key Indicators of the Labour Market (Table 8A). 31 January 2005.

Table II.3.3. Unemployment – Female 1990, 1995, 1999-2003

(per cent of total labour force)

	1990	1995	1999	2000	2001	2002	2003	avg. 99-03
East Asia								
China	...	...	...	...	...	...	...	...
Korea, Rep. of	1.8	1.7	5.1	3.3	3.1	2.5	3.1	3.4
Mongolia	...	6.7	5.3	5.0	5.1	3.8	3.8	4.6
South-East Asia								
Cambodia	...	...	...	2.8	2.2	...	...	2.5
Indonesia	...	...	...	...	...	...	...	...
Lao PDR	...	...	...	...	...	...	...	...
Malaysia	...	3.8	3.3	3.1	3.8	3.8	3.6	3.5
Myanmar	...	...	...	...	...	...	...	...
Philippines	9.8	9.4	9.3	9.9	10.3	...	...	9.8
Singapore	1.3	2.8	4.6	5.1	3.4	5.0	5.3	4.7
Timor-Leste	...	...	...	...	...	...	...	...
Thailand	2.4	1.4	3.0	2.3	2.5	1.6	1.4	2.2
Viet Nam	...	...	...	...	3.2	...	...	3.2
South Asia								
Afghanistan	...	...	...	...	...	...	...	...
Bangladesh	1.9	...	...	3.3	...	...	...	3.3
India[a]	...	1.7	...	4.3	...	...	...	4.3
Iran, Islamic Rep. of	...	...	...	4.5	4.0	4.1	...	4.2
Nepal	...	...	0.7	...	...	...	...	0.7
Pakistan	0.9	13.7	15.0	17.3	17.3	16.5	...	16.5
Sri Lanka	23.5	19.7	12.6	11.1	11.7	12.8	14.6	12.6
Pacific Islands								
Fiji	...	...	...	...	...	...	...	...
Kiribati	...	...	...	...	...	...	...	...
Papua New Guinea	5.9	...	...	1.3	...	...	...	1.3
Solomon Islands	...	...	...	...	...	...	...	...
Vanuatu	...	...	...	...	...	...	...	...
Developed (Industrialized) Economies								
Australia	7.2	7.9	6.8	6.2	6.6	6.2	6.2	6.4
Japan	2.2	3.2	4.5	4.5	4.7	5.1	4.9	4.7
New Zealand	7.2	6.3	6.5	5.8	5.3	5.3	5.0	5.6

Note: Australia: 1995: estimates based on population census; Bangladesh: 1995 column shows data for 1996: persons aged 10 and over; Korea, Rep. of: 1992, 2000: population census: Pakistan: 1990: computed from 87-88 survey results; Singapore: 1990, 2000: population census, Sri Lanka: 1990, 2003: whole country Laborsta data has been supplemented by data on unemployment rate from ADB, *Asian Development Outlook 2005* (Table A6).

Source: Laborsta-on-line (Table 3A), [a]ILO 2003-2004 Key Indicators of the Labour Market (Table 8A). 31 January 2005.

Table II.4.1. Youth unemployment – 1990, 1995, 2000-2003

	1990		1995		2000		2001		2002		2003	
	Youth unemployed ('000)	Youth unemploy-ment rate (%)	Youth unemployed ('000)	Youth unemploy-ment rate (%)	Youth unemployed ('000)	Youth unemploy-ment rate (%)	Youth unemployed ('000)	Youth unemploy-ment rate (%)	Youth unemployed ('000)	Youth unemploy-ment rate (%)	Youth unemployed ('000)	Youth unemploy-ment rate (%)
East Asia												
China	3 832.0	2.5	5 196.0	2.9	5 950.0	3.1	...	...	...	...	...	...
Korea, Rep. of	185.0	7.0	173.0	6.3	232.0	10.2	219.0	9.7	184.0	8.1	213	9.6
Mongolia	...	...	...	...	...	...	...	...	...	...	...	...
South-East Asia												
Cambodia	...	...	...	...	80.6	...	62.1	...	...	...	...	...
Indonesia[a]	1 546.4	...	2 627.6	13.4	...	...	...	...	...	...	...	...
Lao PDR	...	...	...	...	...	...	...	...	...	...	...	...
Malaysia	...	...	179.6	...	186.3	8.3	226.2	...	228	...	240.6	...
Myanmar	...	...	...	...	...	...	...	...	...	...	...	...
Philippines	947.0	15.4	1 086.0	16.1	1 480.0	21.2	1 489.0	19.0	...	...	1 357.0	13.3
Singapore[b]	12.4	4.3	14.3	5.0	14.8	4.7	16.4	...	21.4	...	19.8	...
Timor-Leste	...	...	...	...	...	...	...	...	...	...	...	...
Thailand[a]	403.8	4.3	172.5	2.5	401.3	6.6	...	...	338.7	...	290.4	5.0
Viet Nam	...	...	...	...	...	...	...	...	...	...	...	...
South Asia												
Afghanistan	...	...	...	...	...	...	...	...	...	...	...	...
Bangladesh	...	...	...	...	1 388.0	10.7	...	...	...	...	...	...
India	...	...	...	...	...	...	...	...	...	...	...	...
Iran, Islamic Rep. of	...	...	...	...	...	...	...	...	...	...	...	...
Nepal	...	...	...	...	...	...	...	...	...	...	...	...
Pakistan	419.0	5.1	729.0	8.9	1 357.0	13.3	1 381.0	...	1 609	13.4	...	...
Sri Lanka	591.8	33.3	414.5	32.8	330.4	23.6	356.0	...	387.1	...	437.0	27.2
Pacific Islands												
Fiji	...	...	...	...	...	...	...	...	...	...	...	...
Kiribati	...	...	...	...	...	...	...	...	...	...	...	...
Papua New Guinea	...	...	...	...	32.1	5.3	...	...	...	...	...	...
Solomon Islands	...	...	...	...	...	...	...	...	...	...	...	...
Vanuatu	...	...	...	...	...	...	...	...	...	...	...	...
Developed (Industrialized) Economies												
Australia	253.8	13.2	269.0	14.4	211.5	11.8	235.9	12.9	232.7	12.7	215.2	11.6
Japan	360.0	4.3	540.0	6.1	700.0	9.2	710.0	9.7	700.0	10.1	680.0	10.1
New Zealand	52.6	14.1	43.4	11.9	43.7	13.2	40.0	11.8	40.3	11.4	36.7	10.2

Source: (KILM 3rd edition database, ILO) [a] 1996 data is applied for 1995 [b] 1989 data is applied for 1990.

Table II.5.1. Employment by major economic sector – Agriculture 1990, 1995, 1999-2003

(per cent of total employment)

	1990	1995	1999	2000	2001	2002	2003	avg. 99-03
East Asia								
China	64.9	59.3	60.7	60.6	60.1	56.6	...	59.5
Korea, Rep. of	17.9	12.4	11.6	10.6	10.0	9.3	8.8	10.1
Mongolia	...	46.1	49.5	48.6	48.3	44.9	41.8	46.6
South-East Asia								
Cambodia[b]	...	...	...	73.7	70.2	...	...	...
Indonesia	56.0	44.0	43.2	45.5	44.3	44.3	...	44.3
Lao PDR[a]	78.1	...	...	...	...	...	...	...
Malaysia	26.0	20.0	18.4	18.4	15.1	14.9	14.3	16.2
Myanmar	69.7	...	...	...	...	...	...	...
Philippines	45.2	44.1	37.8	37.5	37.4	...	...	37.6
Singapore	...	0.2	0.3	0.2	0.3	0.3	0.2	0.3
Timor-Leste[a]	83.6	...	...	...	...	...	...	...
Thailand	64.0	52.0	48.5	48.8	46.0	46.1	44.9	46.9
Viet Nam[a]	...	69.7	...	...	...	...	...	...
South Asia								
Afghanistan[a]	86.5	...	...	...	...	...	...	...
Bangladesh	69.5	...	...	64.8	...	...	...	64.8
India[a]	69.1	66.7	...	...	...	...	...	...
Iran, Islamic Rep. of[a]	26.4	22.1	...	...	...	...	...	...
Nepal[a]	83.8	74.8	...	...	...	...	...	...
Pakistan	51.2	46.8	47.3	48.4	48.4	42.1	...	46.6
Sri Lanka	48.6	39.6	...	...	...	36.8	35.6	36.2
Pacific Islands								
Fiji[a]	2.6	2.4	...	...	...	...	...	...
Kiribati[a]	13.0	6.1	...	...	...	...	...	...
Papua New Guinea[a]	79.1	...	...	73.3	...	...	...	...
Solomon Islands[a]	...	...	...	...	...	...	...	...
Vanuatu[a]	...	...	...	...	...	...	...	...
Developed (Industrialized) Economies								
Australia	5.6	5.0	5.0	5.0	4.8	4.5	3.9	4.6
Japan	7.3	5.7	5.2	5.1	4.9	4.7	4.7	4.9
New Zealand	10.6	9.7	9.4	8.7	9.1	8.8	8.2	8.8

Source: ILO Laborsta (Table 2B), [a] ILO 2003-2004 KILM, [b] World Bank, *World Development Indicators.* 14 February 2005. Bangladesh: 1996: persons aged 10 years and over; Korea, Rep. of: 1992, 2000: estimates based on population census; New Zealand: 1992, 2000: methodology or classification revised, data not stricly comparable; Singapore: 1990, 2000: based on population census; Sri Lanka: 1990, 2003: whole country; Viet Nam: 1990-1995. Source: LMIL, 1995-1999: Source: ESCAP.

Table II.5.2. Employment by major economic sector – Industry 1990, 1995, 1999-2003

(per cent of total employment)

	1990	1995	1999	2000	2001	2002	2003	avg. 99-03
East Asia								
China	23.0	25.7	22.6	22.7	23.0	22.7	...	22.7
Korea, Rep. of	35.4	33.3	27.5	28.2	27.5	27.3	27.6	27.6
Mongolia	...	18.0	15.5	14.1	13.7	14.3	15.6	14.7
South-East Asia								
Cambodia[a]	...	...	...	8.4	10.5	...	...	...
Indonesia	13.8	18.4	17.8	16.9	17.7	18.8	...	17.8
Lao PDR[a]	6.3	...	...	...	...	...	...	...
Malaysia	27.5	32.3	31.7	32.2	33.1	32.0	32.0	32.2
Myanmar	9.2	...	...	...	...	...	...	...
Philippines	15.0	15.6	16.2	16.0	15.6	...	...	...
Singapore	...	31.2	28.5	34.2	25.4	24.6	24.1	27.4
Timor-Leste[a]	5.2	...	...	...	...	...	...	...
Thailand	14.0	19.8	18.4	19.0	18.8	19.8	19.8	19.2
Viet Nam[a]	...	13.2	...	...	...	...	...	...
South Asia								
Afghanistan[a]	13.1	...	...	...	...	...	...	...
Bangladesh	13.6	...	...	10.7	...	...	...	...
India[a]	13.6	12.9	...	...	...	...	...	...
Iran, Islamic Rep. of[b]	28.3	31.4	...	...	...	...	...	...
Nepal[a]	2.4	5.2	...	...	...	...	...	...
Pakistan	19.8	18.5	17.1	18.0	18.0	20.8	...	18.5
Sri Lanka	20.9	24.8	...	...	...	24.9	24.3	24.6
Pacific Islands								
Fiji[a]	34.5	38.1	...	...	...	...	...	...
Kiribati[a]	21.3	6.4	...	...	...	...	...	...
Papua New Guinea[a]	6.5	...	...	3.7	...	...	...	...
Solomon Islands[a]	...	...	...	...	...	...	...	...
Vanuatu[a]	...	...	...	...	...	...	...	...
Developed (Industrialized) Economies								
Australia	25.1	22.8	21.3	21.7	20.9	21.0	21.0	21.2
Japan	34.2	33.7	31.9	31.4	30.7	29.9	29.5	30.7
New Zealand	24.7	25.1	23.0	23.3	22.8	22.7	22.4	22.8

Source: ILO Laborsta (Table 2B), [a] ILO 2003-2004 KILM, [b] World Bank, *World Development Indicators.* 14 February 2005. Bangladesh: 1996: persons aged 10 years and over; Korea, Rep. of: 1992, 2000: estimates based on population census; New Zealand: 1992, 2000: methodology or classification revised, data not stricly comparable; Singapore: 1990, 2000: based on population census; Sri Lanka: 1990, 2003: whole country; Viet Nam: 1990-1995. Source: LMIL, 1995-1999: Source: ESCAP.

Table II.5.3. Employment by major economic sector – Services 1990, 1995, 1999-2003

(per cent of total employment)

	1990	1995	1999	2000	2001	2002	2003	avg. 99-03
East Asia								
China	12.0	15.0	16.7	16.7	16.9	20.7	...	17.8
Korea, Rep. of	46.7	54.3	61.0	61.2	62.5	63.3	63.5	62.3
Mongolia	...	35.9	35.0	37.2	38.0	40.7	42.6	38.7
South-East Asia								
Cambodia[a]	...	...	...	19.7	19.3	...	...	...
Indonesia	30.3	37.6	38.9	37.5	38.0	36.9	...	37.8
Lao PDR[a]	15.6	...	...	...	...	...	...	...
Malaysia	46.5	47.7	49.9	49.5	51.8	53.1	53.7	51.6
Myanmar	21.1	...	...	...	...	...	...	...
Philippines	39.7	40.3	45.9	46.5	47.0	...	...	...
Singapore	...	68.5	71.2	65.5	74.3	75.1	75.6	72.3
Timor-Leste[a]	11.2	...	...	...	...	...	...	...
Thailand	22.0	28.3	33.1	32.2	35.1	34.0	35.3	34.0
Viet Nam[a]	...	17.0	...	...	...	...	...	...
South Asia								
Afghanistan[a]	0.4	...	...	...	...	...	...	...
Bangladesh	16.9	...	...	24.5	...	...	...	...
India[a]	17.3	20.3	...	...	...	...	...	...
Iran, Islamic Rep. of[b]	45.3	46.5	...	...	...	...	...	...
Nepal[a]	13.8	20.0	...	...	...	...	...	...
Pakistan	29.0	34.6	35.6	33.5	33.5	37.1	...	35.0
Sri Lanka	30.5	35.6	...	...	...	38.3	40.1	39.2
Pacific Islands								
Fiji[a]	62.9	59.5	...	...	...	...	...	...
Kiribati[a]	65.7	87.5	...	...	...	...	...	...
Papua New Guinea[a]	14.3	...	...	23.0	...	...	...	...
Solomon Islands[a]	...	...	...	...	...	...	...	...
Vanuatu[a]	...	...	...	...	...	...	...	...
Developed (Industrialized) Economies								
Australia	69.3	72.2	73.7	73.3	74.3	74.5	75.0	74.2
Japan	58.5	60.6	62.9	63.5	64.4	65.3	65.8	64.4
New Zealand	64.7	65.2	67.6	68.0	68.1	68.5	69.5	68.3

Source: ILO Laborsta (Table 2B), [a] ILO 2003-2004 KILM, [b] World Bank, *World Development Indicators.* 14 February 2005. Bangladesh: 1996: persons aged 10 years and over; Korea, Rep. of:, 1992, 2000: estimates based on population census; New Zealand: 1992, 2000: methodology or classification revised, data not stricly comparable; Singapore: 1990, 2000: based on population census; Sri Lanka: 1990, 2003: whole country; Viet Nam: 1990-1995. Source: LMIL, 1995-1999: Source: ESCAP.

Table II.6.1. Self-employed as per cent of non-agricultural employment 1990/2000

	1990/2000*		
	Both sexes	Male	Female
East Asia			
China	15	...	...
Korea, Rep. of	30	29	32
Mongolia	...	...	...
South-East Asia			
Cambodia	49	39	66
Indonesia	51	...	60
Lao PDR	...	...	...
Malaysia	17	17	17
Myanmar	...	...	...
Philippines	34	28	41
Singapore	13	13	14
Timor-Leste	...	...	...
Thailand	36	...	40
Viet Nam	...	...	...
South Asia			
Afghanistan	...	...	...
Bangladesh	75	73	83
India	37	38	41
Iran, Islamic Rep. of	37	37	39
Nepal	...	...	...
Pakistan	43	44	34
Sri Lanka	...	...	...
Pacific Islands			
Fiji	...	...	...
Kiribati	...	...	...
Papua New Guinea	...	...	...
Solomon Islands	...	...	...
Vanuatu	...	...	...
Developed (Industrialized) Economies			
Australia	9	11	7
Japan	14	12	16
New Zealand	16	21	11

Note: * Data is provided for one year for which it was available in the period 1990-2000.

Source: *Women and Men in the Informal Economy: A Statistical Picture,* Annexe 2, Working paper – Employment Sector, ILO, Geneva 2002.

Table III.1.1. Manufacturing wage indices 1990, 1995, 1999-2001

(1990 = 100)

	1990	1995	1999	2000	2001
East Asia					
China	100.0	129.2	179.0	200.7	...
Korea, Rep. of	100.0	140.8	155.6	165.2	168.6
Mongolia	...	62.2	...	...	...
South-East Asia					
Cambodia	...	...	...	...	...
Indonesia	100.0	172.4	160.9	...	...
Lao PDR	...	...	...	...	...
Malaysia	100.0	125.1	...	148.4	161.4
Myanmar	...	...	...	...	...
Philippines	100.0	100.6	77.3	78.3	...
Singapore	100.0	136.3	171.6	183.4	186.5
Timor-Leste	...	...	...	...	...
Thailand	100.0	117.7	114.9	...	...
Viet Nam	...	...	...	...	...
South Asia					
Afghanistan	...	...	...	...	...
Bangladesh	...	...	...	...	...
India	100.0	74.5	68.7	...	...
Iran, Islamic Rep. of	100.0	...	...	...	...
Nepal	100.0	...	...	...	...
Pakistan	100.0	100.7	71.5	71.2	...
Sri Lanka	100.0	108.6	102.3	107.6	97.7
Pacific Islands					
Fiji	100.0	...	...	...	...
Kiribati	...	...	...	...	...
Papua New Guinea	...	...	...	...	...
Solomon Islands	100.0	87.5	...	...	...
Vanuatu	...	...	...	...	...
Developed (Industrialized) Economies					
Australia	100.0	102.3	107.8	108.0	108.3
Japan	100.0	111.9	116.5	116.5	117.9
New Zealand	100.0	99.2	107.4	107.6	108.3

Note: ... indicates that the data is not available.
Source: KILM (Table 15), 23 February 2005.

Table III.2.1. Hours of work per week 1990, 1995, 1999-2003

	1990	1995	1999	2000	2001	2002	2003	avg. 99-03
East Asia								
China	...	...	...	...	...	...	...	...
Korea, Rep. of	48.2	47.7	47.9	47.5	47.0	46.2	45.9	46.9
Mongolia	...	...	...	...	...	...	...	...
South-East Asia								
Cambodia	...	...	...	...	...	...	...	...
Indonesia	...	...	...	...	...	...	...	...
Lao PDR	...	...	...	...	...	...	...	...
Malaysia	...	...	...	...	...	...	...	...
Myanmar	...	...	...	...	...	...	...	...
Philippines	47.6	42.0	42.2	42.1	40.1	39.9	41.1	41.1
Singapore	46.5	47.1	46.8	47.0	46.2	46.0	46.0	46.4
Timor-Leste	...	...	...	...	...	...	...	...
Thailand	...	...	...	50.1	42.4	...	...	46.3
Viet Nam	...	...	46.2	46.8	43.9	43.6	44.1	44.9
South Asia								
Afghanistan	...	...	...	...	...	...	...	...
Bangladesh	59.0	51.0	...	32.0	...	...	...	32.0
India	47.8	45.5	47.6	47.5	46.7	...	...	47.3
Iran, Islamic Rep. of	...	...	...	...	...	...	...	...
Nepal	...	...	...	...	...	...	...	...
Pakistan	...	...	...	...	...	...	...	...
Sri Lanka	...	...	...	...	...	...	...	...
Pacific Islands								
Fiji	...	...	...	...	...	...	...	...
Kiribati	...	...	...	...	...	...	...	...
Papua New Guinea	...	...	...	...	...	...	...	...
Solomon Islands	...	...	...	...	...	...	...	...
Vanuatu	...	...	...	...	...	...	...	...
Developed (Industrialized) Economies								
Australia	35.8	35.9	35.7	35.6	35.2	34.9	34.8	35.2
Japan	45.7	43.4	42.3	42.7	42.2	42.2	42.0	42.3
New Zealand	...	...	34.8	34.4	34.4	34.4	34.4	34.5

Note: ... indicates that the data is not available.

Source: Laborsta. Australia: hours actually worked, labour force survey, employees. 2000: data not stricly comparable due to changes in coding methods. Bangladesh: hours actually worked, labour force survey, total employment (without agriculture and fishing). India: hours actually worked, administrative reports, employee's (without agriculture). Japan: hours actually worked, labour force survey, total employment. Korea, Rep. of: hours actually worked, employees, labour related establishment survey. New Zealand: hours actually worked, employees, labour force survey.

Table III.3.1. Excessive* hours of work per week 1990, 1995, 1999-2003

	1990	1995	1999	2000	2001	2002	2003
East Asia							
China	...	...	...	...	...	...	...
Korea, Rep. of	51.9	47.2	42.2	42.5	42.1	40.1	38.1
Mongolia	...	...	...	...	...	...	36.1
South-East Asia							
Cambodia	...	...	...	...	43.0	...	...
Indonesia	...	...	16.0	15.9	17.2	15.8	15.4
Lao PDR	...	...	...	...	...	...	...
Malaysia	...	...	...	...	...	...	...
Myanmar	...	...	...	...	...	...	...
Philippines	...	...	21.6	24.0	21.5	22.2	...
Singapore	...	...	...	...	35.0	34.7	36.5
Timor-Leste	...	...	...	...	...	...	...
Thailand	56.2	53.8	48.6	50.1	38.1	37.2	39.6
Viet Nam	...	...	28.8	34.3	25.6	23.5	23.8
South Asia							
Afghanistan	...	...	...	...	...	...	...
Bangladesh	...	...	...	31.7	...	...	...
India	...	...	...	...	...	...	...
Iran, Islamic Rep. of	...	...	...	...	...	...	...
Nepal	...	...	...	...	...	...	...
Pakistan	...	...	...	...	42.8	...	...
Sri Lanka	...	...	...	...	...	27.4	...
Pacific Islands							
Fiji	...	...	...	...	...	...	...
Kiribati	...	...	...	...	...	...	...
Papua New Guinea	...	...	...	...	...	...	...
Solomon Islands	...	...	...	...	...	...	...
Vanuatu	...	...	...	...	...	...	...
Developed (Industrialized) Economies							
Australia	...	...	20.0	19.8	19.1	18.7	18.5
Japan	...	28.7	27.3	28.8	27.5	28.9	29.0
New Zealand	...	...	...	...	...	...	...

* *Definition:* Employed persons working 50 hours or more per week as a percentage of total employment.

Source: Computed by Anne Chataignier (ILO/SDA, Geneva) from Labour Force Surveys data.

Table IV.1.1. Poverty and income distribution

	Population in Poverty (%) (National Poverty Line)[a]				Proportion of Population Below (PPP) $1 a Day (%)		Proportion of Population Below (PPP) $2 a Day (%)		Gini Coefficient[b]	
	Total	Urban	Rural	Year	Value	Year	Value	Year	Value	Year
East Asia										
China	...	...	3.1	2003	16.6	2001	46.7	2001	0.447	2001
Korea, Rep. of	3.6	...	...	2000	<0.5	2002	<0.5	2002	0.352	2000
Mongolia	35.6	39.4	32.6	1998	27.0	1998	74.9	1998	0.303	1998
South-East Asia										
Cambodia	35.9	18.2	40.1	1999	34.1	1997	77.7	1997	0.450	1999
Indonesia	18.2	14.5	21.1	2002	7.5	2002	52.4	2002	0.343	2002
Lao PDR	38.6	26.9	41.0	1997	39.0	1997	81.7	1997	0.370	1997
Malaysia	7.5	3.4	12.4	1999	<0.5	1997	9.3	1997	0.440	1999
Myanmar	22.9	23.9	22.4	1997	...	...	...	...	...	...
Philippines	34.0	20.4	47.4	2000	15.5	2000	47.5	2000	0.461	2000
Singapore	...	...	...	...	...	...	...	...	0.425	1998
Timor-Leste	41.0	26.0	46.0	2001	...	...	...	...	0.354	2001
Thailand	9.8	4.0	12.6	2002	1.9	2000	32.5	2002	0.432	2000
Viet Nam	28.9	6.6	35.6	2002	13.1	2002	58.5	2002	0.376	2002
South Asia										
Afghanistan	...	...	...	...	...	...	...	...	...	...
Bangladesh	49.8	36.6	53.0	2000	36.0	2000	82.8	2000	0.318	2000
India	26.1	23.6	27.1	1999	36.0	1999	81.3	1999	0.325	1999
Iran, Islamic Rep. of	...	...	...	...	...	...	...	...	...	...
Nepal	42.0	23.0	44.0	1996	39.1	1995	80.9	1995	0.367	1995
Pakistan	32.6	25.9	34.8	1999	25.3	1996	77.2	1996	0.330	1998
Sri Lanka	25.2	14.7	27.0	1995	6.6	1995	45.4	1995	0.344	1995
Pacific Islands										
Fiji	25.5	27.6	22.4	1990	25.0	1990	...	...	0.490	1990
Kiribati	...	...	...	...	38.0	1996	...	...	...	...
Papua New Guinea	37.5	16.1	41.3	1996	24.6	1996	54.4	1996	0.480	1996
Solomon Islands	...	...	...	...	...	...	...	...	...	...
Vanuatu	...	...	...	...	40.0	1998	...	...	...	...

Note: ... indicates that the data is not available.

[a] When available, official poverty lines are used. In some countries, no official poverty line is available, and data may have been computed by non-governmental agencies.

[b] Calculated based on income or expenditure.

Source: Asian Development Bank, *Key Indicators of Developing Asian and Pacific Countries 2004.* (Special Chapter on Poverty, Table 9) ESCAP, *Economic and Social Survey of Asia and the Pacific 2004* (Table III.2) for supplementary data.

Table IV.2.1. Economically active children (aged 10-14 years) 1990, 1995, 1999-2003

(as per cent of age group)

	1990	1995	1999	2000	2001	2002	2003	avg. 99-03
East Asia								
China	15.2	11.6	8.6	7.9	7.1	5.7	4.0	6.6
Korea, Rep. of	0.0	0.0	0.0	0.0	0.0	0.0	0.0	0.0
Mongolia	2.5	1.9	1.5	1.4	1.2	1.0	0.7	1.1
South-East Asia								
Cambodia	25.6	24.7	23.9	23.7	23.6	23.4	23.2	23.6
Indonesia	11.3	9.6	8.2	7.8	7.5	7.1	6.8	7.5
Lao PDR	29.1	27.2	25.7	25.4	25.0	24.6	24.3	25.0
Malaysia	4.0	3.2	2.5	2.3	2.1	1.7	1.2	2.0
Myanmar	26.1	24.5	23.3	22.9	22.6	22.3	22.0	22.6
Philippines	10.6	8.0	6.0	5.4	4.9	3.9	2.7	4.6
Singapore	0.0	0.0	0.0	0.0	0.0	0.0	0.0	0.0
Timor-Leste	39.9	38.1	36.6	36.3	35.9	35.5	35.2	35.9
Thailand	20.2	16.2	13.0	12.2	11.5	10.8	10.0	11.5
Viet Nam	13.0	9.1	6.0	5.2	4.7	3.8	2.6	4.5
South Asia								
Afghanistan	26.3	25.3	24.4	24.2	24.0	23.8	23.5	24.0
Bangladesh	32.5	30.1	28.2	27.7	27.3	26.9	26.5	27.4
India	16.7	14.4	12.5	12.1	11.6	11.2	10.7	11.6
Iran, Islamic Rep. of	6.8	4.7	3.0	2.6	2.3	1.9	1.3	2.2
Nepal	48.3	45.2	42.7	42.1	41.4	40.8	40.2	41.4
Pakistan	20.1	17.7	15.9	15.4	14.9	14.4	14.0	14.9
Sri Lanka	2.9	2.4	2.1	2.0	1.8	1.4	1.0	1.7
Pacific Islands								
Fiji	...	...	...	...	...	...	...	...
Kiribati	...	...	...	...	...	...	...	...
Papua New Guinea	21.5	19.3	17.6	17.2	16.8	16.4	16.0	16.8
Solomon Islands	33.6	28.9	25.2	24.2	23.3	22.4	21.4	23.3
Vanuatu	...	...	...	...	...	...	...	...
Developed (Industrialized) Economies								
Australia	0.0	0.0	0.0	0.0	0.0	0.0	0.0	0.0
Japan	0.0	0.0	0.0	0.0	0.0	0.0	0.0	0.0
New Zealand	0.0	0.0	0.0	0.0	0.0	0.0	0.0	0.0

Note: ... indicates that the data is not available.

Source: World Bank, *World Development Indicators.* 12 January 2005.

Table IV.3.1. Share of labour force belonging to a trade union 1990, 1995-2003

(per cent)

	1990	1995	1996	1997	1998	1999	2000	2001	2002	2003
East Asia										
China	15.1	14.4	14.0	12.4	12.0	11.6	13.7	...	...	...
Korea, Rep. of	9.6	7.3	7.1	6.5	6.0	6.3	6.4	6.5	6.5	...
Mongolia	...	...	...	...	...	...	...	...	...	...
South-East Asia										
Cambodia	...	...	...	...	...	...	...	...	...	...
Indonesia	...	1.1	...	...	...	...	...	...	...	...
Lao PDR	...	...	...	...	...	...	...	...	...	...
Malaysia	9.2	8.6	8.6	8.4	8.2	7.8	7.6	7.9	...	...
Myanmar	...	...	...	...	...	...	...	...	...	...
Philippines	12.4	12.8	12.5	12.2	12.1	11.9	11.7	11.6	11.4	...
Singapore	13.6	13.1	13.8	13.6	13.9	14.7	15.8	16.6	19.0	...
Timor-Leste	...	...	...	...	...	...	...	...	...	...
Thailand	...	1.2	...	...	...	0.3	...	...	4.2	...
Viet Nam	...	...	...	...	...	...	...	...	...	...
South Asia										
Afghanistan	...	...	...	...	...	...	...	...	...	...
Bangladesh	3.2	2.9	2.8	2.8	2.8	2.8	2.8	2.7	2.8	...
India	1.9	1.6	1.4	1.8	...	...	...	...	...	...
Iran, Islamic Rep. of	...	...	...	...	...	...	...	...	...	...
Nepal	...	...	...	...	...	...	...	...	...	...
Pakistan	...	...	...	...	...	...	...	...	...	...
Sri Lanka	13.8	19.9	17.1	11.7	10.4	10.2	...	...	...	...
Pacific Islands										
Fiji	...	...	...	...	...	...	...	...	...	...
Kiribati	...	...	...	...	...	...	...	...	...	...
Papua New Guinea	...	...	...	...	...	...	...	...	...	...
Solomon Islands	...	...	...	...	...	...	...	...	...	...
Vanuatu	...	...	...	...	...	...	...	...	...	...
Developed (Industrialized) Economies										
Australia	31.3	24.7	23.7	22.4	21.4	19.4	19.4	19.2	18.3	18.4
Japan	19.1	18.8	18.5	18.2	17.8	17.4	16.9	16.5	15.9	...
New Zealand	36.3	20.0	18.4	17.5	16.2	15.8	16.5	17.0	17.0	...

Note: ... indicates that the data is not available.

Source: ILO-compiled database, Policy Integration Department, 2004.

Table IV.4.1. Ratification of ILO Conventions

	Freedom of association and collective bargaining		Elimination of forced and compulsory labour		Elimination of discrimination in respect of employment and occupation		Abolition of child labour		Total No. of ILO Conventions ratified
	C. 87[a]	C. 98[b]	C. 29[c]	C. 105[d]	C. 100[e]	C. 111[f]	C. 138[g]	C. 182[h]	
Afghanistan				●	●	●			15
Australia	●	●	●	●	●	●			58
Bangladesh	●	●	●	●	●	●		●	33
Cambodia	●	●	●	●	●	●	●		12
China					●		●	●	23
Fiji	●	●	●	●	●	●	●	●	25
India			●	●	●	●			41
Indonesia	●	●	●	●	●	●	●	●	17
Iran, Islamic Rep. of			●	●	●	●		●	12
Japan	●	●	●		●		●	●	46
Kiribati	●	●	●	●					4
Korea, Rep. of					●	●	●	●	20
Lao PDR			●				●	●	6
Malaysia		●	●	◆	●		●	●	34
Mongolia	●	●	●	●	●	●	●	●	16
Myanmar	●		●						21
Nepal		●	●		●	●	●	●	9
New Zealand		●	●	●	●	●		●	59
Pakistan	●	●	●	●	●	●		●	34
Papua New Guinea	●	●	●	●	●	●	●	●	26
Philippines	●	●		●	●	●	●	●	31
Singapore		●	●	◆	●			●	23
Solomon Islands			●						14
Sri Lanka	●	●	●	●	●	●	●	●	40
Thailand			●	●	●		●	●	14
Timor-Leste									0
Vanuatu									0
Viet Nam					●	●	●	●	16
Asia: Total Ratifications	**13**	**16**	**21**	**16**	**22**	**17**	**14**	**18**	**649**
Asia (percentage of total ratifications)	9.09	10.39	12.73	9.82	13.66	10.56	10.29	11.76	23.18

Note: ● Convention ratified ◆ Convention denounced

[a] Freedom of Association and Protection of the Right to Organize Convention (1948).
[b] Right to Organize and Collective Bargaining Convention (1949).
[c] Forced Labour Convention (1930).
[d] Abolition of Forced Labour Convention (1957).
[e] Equal Remuneration Convention (1951).
[f] Discrimination (Employment and Occupation) Convention (1958).
[g] Minimum Age Convention (1973).
[h] Worst Forms of Child Labour Convention (1999).

Source: ILO Database on International Labour Standards (ILOLEX). [http://www.ilo.org/ilolex/english/docs/declworld.htm]. 11 May 2005.

Table V.1.1. Gross domestic product (annual growth rate) 1990, 1995, 1999-2003

(per cent)

	1990	1995	1999	2000	2001	2002	2003	avg. 99-03
East Asia								
China	3.8	10.5	7.1	8.0	7.5	8.0	9.1	7.9
Korea, Rep. of	9.0	10.4	9.5	8.5	3.8	7.0	3.1	6.4
Mongolia	-2.5	6.3	3.2	1.1	1.4	4.0	4.7	2.9
South-East Asia								
Cambodia	...	6.9	10.8	7.0	5.7	5.5	7.6	7.3
Indonesia	9.0	8.4	0.8	4.9	3.4	3.7	4.1	3.4
Lao PDR	6.7	7.0	7.3	5.8	5.7	5.0	5.0	5.8
Malaysia	9.0	9.8	6.1	8.5	0.3	4.2	5.2	4.9
Myanmar	2.8	6.9	10.9	13.7	9.7	...	...	11.5
Philippines	3.0	4.7	3.4	6.0	3.0	4.4	4.5	4.3
Singapore	9.0	8.0	6.4	9.4	-2.4	3.3	1.1	3.6
Timor-Leste	...	...	-35.5	15.5	15.0	2.0	-2.0	-1.0
Thailand	11.2	9.2	4.4	4.8	2.1	5.4	6.7	4.7
Viet Nam	5.1	9.5	4.8	6.8	6.9	7.0	7.2	6.5
South Asia								
Afghanistan	...	...	...	...	...	...	...	...
Bangladesh	5.9	4.9	4.9	5.9	5.3	4.4	5.3	5.2
India	5.8	7.6	7.1	3.9	5.2	4.6	8.0	5.8
Iran, Islamic Rep. of	11.2	2.9	2.5	5.9	5.3	7.2	5.9	5.4
Nepal	4.5	3.3	4.5	6.1	5.5	-0.6	3.0	3.7
Pakistan	4.5	5.0	3.7	4.3	2.6	2.8	5.8	3.8
Sri Lanka	6.4	5.5	4.3	6.0	-1.5	4.0	5.5	3.6
Pacific Islands								
Fiji	4.4	2.5	9.5	-3.2	3.1	4.1	5.0	3.7
Kiribati	2.1	5.4	9.8	1.5	1.5	1.4	1.4	3.1
Papua New Guinea	-3.0	-3.3	7.6	-1.2	-2.3	-0.6	2.5	1.2
Solomon Islands	1.8	7.0	-1.3	-13.4	-10.0	-2.7	3.8	-4.7
Vanuatu	0.0	0.0	-2.1	2.5	-1.9	-0.3	2.0	0.0
Developed (Industrialized) Economies								
Australia	-0.1	4.2	4.0	1.8	3.9	2.7	2.4	3.0
Japan	5.2	1.9	0.1	2.8	0.4	0.3	2.7	1.3
New Zealand	0.0	4.1	5.0	2.7	3.5	4.3	2.7	3.6

Source: World Bank, *World Development Indicators*, WDI on-line, 25 January 2005.

Table V.1.2. Gross domestic product per capita 1990, 1995, 1999-2003

	1990	1995	1999	2000	2001	2002	2003	avg. 99-03
East Asia								
China	350	581	770	825	880	944	1 024	888
Korea, Rep. of	8 310	11 493	12 668	13 628	14 051	14 937	15 291	14 115
Mongolia	489	392	427	428	430	442	457	437
South-East Asia								
Cambodia	...	316	350	368	381	395	418	382
Indonesia	777	1 049	980	1 015	1 036	1 060	1 090	1 036
Lao PDR	321	376	436	451	465	477	490	464
Malaysia	3 104	4 310	4 541	4 808	4 715	4 811	4 965	4 768
Myanmar	...	...	...	...	...	...	...	...
Philippines	1 091	1 085	1 133	1 173	1 182	1 209	1 239	1 187
Singapore	17 899	23 804	26 295	28 296	26 869	27 533	27 270	27 253
Timor-Leste	...	...	...	...	...	...	...	...
Thailand	1 997	2 865	2 721	2 828	2 866	3 000	3 182	2 919
Viet Nam	211	284	351	370	390	413	438	392
South Asia								
Afghanistan	...	...	...	...	...	...	...	...
Bangladesh	278	316	358	373	386	396	410	385
India	324	381	453	463	479	493	525	483
Iran, Islamic Rep. of	1 291	1 482	1 587	1 658	1 723	1 819	1 899	1 737
Nepal	188	215	233	242	249	242	244	242
Pakistan	450	498	509	518	518	521	538	521
Sri Lanka	616	754	863	902	876	899	937	895
Pacific Islands								
Fiji	2 312	2 585	2 707	2 586	2 648	2 736	2 831	2 701
Kiribati	520	575	705	692	687	682	685	690
Papua New Guinea	766	1 018	985	949	906	879	881	920
Solomon Islands	746	843	765	645	565	534	538	609
Vanuatu	1 123	1 353	1 249	1 254	1 205	1 176	1 174	1 212
Developed (Industrialized) Economies								
Australia	18 621	20 635	23 333	23 476	24 109	24 455	24 756	24 025
Japan	39 865	42 282	43 653	44 799	44 924	45 029	46 223	44 926
New Zealand	15 147	16 558	17 553	17 915	18 429	18 947	19 119	18 393

Source: World Bank, *World Development Indicators,* WDI on-line, 12 January 2005.

Table V.1.3. Foreign trade as per cent of gross domestic product 1990, 1995, 1999-2003

(per cent)

	1990	1995	1999	2000	2001	2002	2003	avg. 99-03
East Asia								
China	31.9	45.7	41.5	49.1	48.5	54.8	65.0	51.8
Korea, Rep. of	57.4	58.7	71.4	78.5	73.3	69.1	73.8	73.2
Mongolia	76.9	128.0	135.8	147.4	144.1	148.2	147.9	144.7
South-East Asia								
Cambodia	18.9	79.9	89.2	113.9	118.9	126.6	...	112.1
Indonesia	49.1	54.0	62.9	76.4	77.1	65.1	56.9	67.7
Lao PDR	35.8	60.6	...	...	...	...	...	...
Malaysia	147.0	192.1	217.6	229.3	214.5	210.7	204.8	215.4
Myanmar	7.5	3.1	...	...	...	...	...	...
Philippines	60.8	80.5	102.8	108.9	100.3	98.4	99.0	101.9
Singapore								
Timor-Leste								
Thailand	75.8	90.4	104.0	124.9	125.4	122.2	122.3	119.8
Viet Nam	81.3	74.7	102.8	112.5	111.6	115.0	...	110.5
South Asia								
Afghanistan	...	...	...	...	...	145.6	...	145.6
Bangladesh	19.7	28.2	31.9	33.2	36.9	33.3	34.0	33.9
India	15.7	23.2	25.5	28.5	27.6	30.8	31.8	28.8
Iran, Islamic Rep. of	45.5	39.0	40.8	38.2	48.3	57.3	53.3	47.6
Nepal	32.2	59.5	52.6	55.7	53.8	44.8	43.2	50.0
Pakistan	38.9	36.1	32.3	34.3	37.3	37.7	40.8	36.5
Sri Lanka	67.2	81.6	78.8	88.6	80.9	79.0	77.3	80.9
Pacific Islands								
Fiji	129.5	113.0	124.1	125.1	138.7	...	...	129.3
Kiribati	158.9	104.6	113.8	94.1	...	...	...	104.0
Papua New Guinea	89.6	105.6	90.0	...	...	...	...	90.0
Solomon Islands	119.6	...	...	...	...	...	...	...
Vanuatu	126.2	100.6	107.4	...	...	...	...	107.4
Developed (Industrialized) Economies								
Australia	33.5	39.8	42.4	45.7	43.0	41.8	...	43.2
Japan	19.8	16.7	18.5	20.1	20.1	21.0	...	19.9
New Zealand	53.8	57.8	63.4	70.8	68.2	64.8	...	66.8

Source: World Bank, *World Development Indicators*, WDI on-line, 12 January 2005.

Table V.2.1. Population size 1990, 1995, 1999-2003

(thousand)

	1990	1995	1999	2000	2001	2002	2003	avg. 99-03
East Asia								
China	1 135 185	1 204 855	1 253 735	1 262 645	1 271 850	1 280 400	1 288 400	1 271 406
Korea, Rep. of	42 869	45 093	46 617	47 008	47 343	47 640	47 912	47 304
Mongolia	2 106	2 275	2 378	2 398	2 421	2 449	2 480	2 425
South-East Asia								
Cambodia	9 145	10 695	12 450	12 695	12 936	13 172	13 404	12 931
Indonesia	178 232	192 750	203 568	206 265	208 981	211 716	214 471	209 000
Lao PDR	4 132	4 686	5 158	5 279	5 403	5 530	5 660	5 406
Malaysia	18 202	20 610	22 710	23 270	23 802	24 305	24 774	23 772
Myanmar	40 506	44 094	46 900	47 554	48 183	48 786	49 362	48 157
Philippines	61 040	68 341	74 878	76 627	78 317	79 944	81 503	78 254
Singapore	3 047	3 526	3 952	4 018	4 131	4 164	4 250	4 103
Timor-Leste	740	840	788	737	753	780	810	774
Thailand	55 595	58 610	60 246	60 728	61 184	61 613	62 014	61 157
Viet Nam	66 200	72 980	77 515	78 523	79 493	80 424	81 314	79 454
South Asia								
Afghanistan	17 685	21 930	25 869	26 550	27 259	27 997	28 766	27 288
Bangladesh	110 025	120 130	128 797	131 050	133 345	135 684	138 066	133 388
India	849 515	932 180	999 016	1 015 923	1 032 473	1 048 641	1 064 399	1 032 090
Iran, Islamic Rep. of	54 400	58 954	62 736	63 664	64 528	65 540	66 392	64 572
Nepal	18 142	20 439	22 498	23 043	23 586	24 125	24 660	23 582
Pakistan	107 975	122 375	134 790	138 080	141 450	144 902	148 439	141 532
Sri Lanka	16 267	17 280	18 208	18 467	18 732	19 007	19 193	18 721
Pacific Islands								
Fiji	736	770	801	812	817	823	835	818
Kiribati	72	80	88	91	93	95	96	93
Papua New Guinea	3 980	4 520	5 006	5 130	5 254	5 378	5 502	5 254
Solomon Islands	319	367	408	419	431	443	457	432
Vanuatu	147	168	193	197	201	206	210	201
Developed (Industrialized) Economies								
Australia	17 065	18 063	18 967	19 182	19 414	19 663	19 890	19 423
Japan	123 537	125 439	126 650	126 870	127 037	127 150	127 210	126 983
New Zealand	3 448	3 673	3 835	3 858	3 881	3 939	4 009	3 904

Source: World Bank, *World Development Indicators*, WDI on-line, 15 March 2005.

Table V.2.2. Population growth rate 1991, 1995, 1999-2003

(annual per cent growth)

	1991	1995	1999	2000	2001	2002	2003	avg. 99-03
East Asia								
China	1.4	1.1	1.0	0.7	0.7	0.7	0.6	0.7
Korea, Rep. of	0.9	1.4	0.7	0.8	0.7	0.6	0.6	0.7
Mongolia	1.7	1.4	0.9	0.8	1.0	1.2	1.3	1.0
South-East Asia								
Cambodia	3.2	3.2	2.2	2.0	1.9	1.8	1.8	1.9
Indonesia	1.7	1.4	1.3	1.3	1.3	1.3	1.3	1.3
Lao PDR	2.6	2.5	2.4	2.3	2.3	2.4	2.4	2.4
Malaysia	2.5	2.5	2.4	2.5	2.3	2.1	1.9	2.2
Myanmar	1.7	1.7	1.5	1.4	1.3	1.3	1.2	1.3
Philippines	2.3	2.3	2.3	2.3	2.2	2.1	2.0	2.2
Singapore	2.9	3.1	0.7	1.7	2.8	0.8	2.1	1.6
Timor-Leste	3.0	0.8	-3.8	-6.5	2.2	3.6	3.8	-0.1
Thailand	1.5	0.6	0.8	0.8	0.8	0.7	0.7	0.7
Viet Nam	2.1	1.8	1.3	1.3	1.2	1.2	1.1	1.2
South Asia								
Afghanistan	3.0	5.8	3.3	2.6	2.7	2.7	2.7	2.8
Bangladesh	1.8	1.8	1.8	1.7	1.8	1.8	1.8	1.8
India	2.0	1.8	1.7	1.7	1.6	1.6	1.5	1.6
Iran, Islamic Rep. of	1.6	1.6	1.4	1.5	1.4	1.6	1.3	1.4
Nepal	2.4	2.4	2.4	2.4	2.4	2.3	2.2	2.3
Pakistan	2.6	2.5	2.4	2.4	2.4	2.4	2.4	2.4
Sri Lanka	1.1	1.1	1.5	1.4	1.4	1.5	1.0	1.4
Pacific Islands								
Fiji	1.2	0.7	1.3	1.4	0.6	0.7	1.5	1.1
Kiribati	2.8	2.6	2.3	3.4	2.2	2.2	1.1	2.2
Papua New Guinea	2.5	2.7	2.5	2.5	2.4	2.4	2.3	2.4
Solomon Islands	3.1	2.5	2.8	2.7	2.9	2.8	3.2	2.9
Vanuatu	3.4	2.4	3.8	2.1	2.0	2.5	1.9	2.5
Developed (Industrialized) Economies								
Australia	1.3	1.2	1.2	1.1	1.2	1.3	1.2	1.2
Japan	0.3	0.4	0.2	0.2	0.1	0.1	0.0	0.1
New Zealand	1.4	1.5	0.5	0.6	0.6	1.5	1.8	1.0

Source: Calculated from WDI data for Table V.2.1.

Table V.3.1. Adult literacy rate – Total 1990, 1995, 1999-2002

(per cent of population ages 15 and above)

	1990	1995	1999	2000	2001	2002	avg. 99-02
East Asia							
China	78.3	81.9	84.5	90.9	...	...	87.7
Korea, Rep. of	>95	>95	>95	>95	>95	>95	...
Mongolia	97.8	98.1	98.4	97.8	...	...	98.1
South-East Asia							
Cambodia	62.0	64.5	67.3	68.0	68.7	69.4	68.4
Indonesia	79.5	83.5	86.2	86.8	87.3	87.9	87.0
Lao PDR	56.5	60.6	63.9	64.8	65.6	66.4	65.2
Malaysia	80.7	84.3	86.8	88.7	...	...	87.7
Myanmar	80.7	82.8	84.3	84.7	85.0	85.3	84.8
Philippines	91.7	93.5	94.6	92.6	...	...	93.6
Singapore	88.8	90.7	91.9	92.5	...	...	92.2
Timor-Leste	...	...	...	...	...	...	...
Thailand	92.4	94.1	95.2	92.6	...	...	93.9
Viet Nam	90.4	91.5	90.3	...	...	...	90.3
South Asia							
Afghanistan	...	...	...	...	...	...	...
Bangladesh	34.2	37.1	39.4	40.0	40.6	41.1	40.3
India	49.3	53.3	56.4	57.2	61.3	...	58.3
Iran, Islamic Rep. of	63.2	70.0	74.8	76.0	77.1	...	76.0
Nepal	30.4	36.0	40.6	41.7	42.9	44.0	42.3
Pakistan	35.4	39.3	...	...	...	...	...
Sri Lanka	88.7	90.2	91.4	91.6	91.9	92.1	91.7
Pacific Islands							
Fiji	88.6	91.0	...	...	...	...	...
Kiribati	...	...	...	...	...	...	...
Papua New Guinea	...	...	...	...	...	...	...
Solomon Islands	...	...	...	...	...	...	...
Vanuatu	...	...	...	...	...	...	...
Developed (Industrialized) Economies							
Australia	>95	>95	>95	>95	>95	>95	>95
Japan	>95	>95	>95	>95	>95	>95	>95
New Zealand	>95	>95	>95	>95	>95	>95	>95

Note: Timor-Leste: On May 20, 2002, Timor-Leste became an independent country. Data for Indonesia include Timor-Leste through 1999 unless otherwise noted.

Source: World Bank, *World Development Indicators,* WDI on-line, 25 January 2005.

Table V.3.2. Adult literacy rate – Male 1990, 1995, 1999-2002

(per cent of population ages 15 and above)

	1990	1995	1999	2000	2001	2002	avg. 99-02
East Asia							
China	87.2	89.9	91.7	95.1	...	...	93.4
Korea, Rep. of	...	...	...	...	...	...	...
Mongolia	98.5	98.5	98.6	98.0	...	...	98.3
South-East Asia							
Cambodia	77.7	78.7	79.8	80.2	80.5	80.8	80.3
Indonesia	86.7	89.6	91.3	91.8	92.1	92.5	91.9
Lao PDR	70.3	73.3	75.6	76.2	76.8	77.4	76.5
Malaysia	86.9	89.3	91.0	92.0	...	...	91.5
Myanmar	87.4	88.2	88.8	88.9	89.1	89.2	89.0
Philippines	92.2	93.8	94.8	92.5	...	...	93.7
Singapore	94.4	95.4	96.1	96.6	...	...	96.3
Timor-Leste	...	...	...	...	...	...	...
Thailand	95.3	96.3	97.0	94.9	...	...	95.9
Viet Nam	94.0	94.2	93.9	...	...	...	93.9
South Asia							
Afghanistan	...	...	...	...	...	...	...
Bangladesh	44.3	46.8	48.9	49.4	49.9	50.3	49.6
India	61.9	65.2	67.7	68.4	...	...	68.0
Iran, Islamic Rep. of	72.2	78.0	82.0	83.0	83.8	83.5	83.1
Nepal	47.4	53.7	58.3	59.4	60.5	61.6	60.0
Pakistan	49.3	53.5	...	...	...	...	...
Sri Lanka	92.9	93.7	94.3	94.4	94.5	94.7	94.5
Pacific Islands							
Fiji	91.6	93.5	...	...	...	...	...
Kiribati	...	...	...	...	...	...	...
Papua New Guinea	...	...	...	...	...	...	...
Solomon Islands	...	...	...	...	...	...	...
Vanuatu	...	...	...	...	...	...	...
Developed (Industrialized) Economies							
Australia	>95	>95	>95	>95	>95	>95	>95
Japan	>95	>95	>95	>95	>95	>95	>95
New Zealand	>95	>95	>95	>95	>95	>95	>95

Note: Timor-Leste: On May 20, 2002, Timor-Leste became an independent country.
Data for Indonesia include Timor-Leste through 1999 unless otherwise noted.

Source: World Bank, *World Development Indicators,* WDI on-line, 25 January 2005.

Table V.3.3. Adult literacy rate – Female 1990, 1995, 1999-2002

(per cent of population ages 15 and above)

	1990	1995	1999	2000	2001	2002	avg. 99-02
East Asia							
China	68.9	73.6	77.0	86.5	...	...	81.8
Korea, Rep. of	...	...	...	...	...	...	...
Mongolia	97.1	97.8	98.2	97.5	...	...	97.8
South-East Asia							
Cambodia	48.8	52.2	56.2	57.2	58.2	59.3	57.7
Indonesia	72.5	77.7	81.1	81.9	82.6	83.4	82.3
Lao PDR	42.8	48.0	52.3	53.4	54.4	55.5	53.9
Malaysia	74.4	79.2	82.5	85.4	...	...	84.0
Myanmar	74.2	77.6	79.9	80.5	81.0	81.4	80.7
Philippines	91.2	93.2	94.5	92.7	...	...	93.6
Singapore	83.2	86.0	87.8	88.6	...	...	88.2
Timor-Leste							
Thailand	89.5	91.9	93.4	90.5	...	...	92.0
Viet Nam	87.1	89.0	86.9	...	...	...	86.9
South Asia							
Afghanistan	...	...	...	...	...	...	...
Bangladesh	23.7	26.9	29.5	30.2	30.8	31.4	30.5
India	35.9	40.6	44.4	45.4	...	...	44.9
Iran, Islamic Rep. of	54.0	61.9	67.5	68.9	70.2	70.4	69.3
Nepal	14.0	18.6	22.9	24.0	25.2	26.4	24.6
Pakistan	20.1	23.8	...	...	...	...	...
Sri Lanka	84.7	86.9	88.6	89.0	89.3	89.6	89.1
Pacific Islands							
Fiji	85.5	88.5	...	...	...	...	...
Kiribati	...	...	...	...	...	...	...
Papua New Guinea	...	...	...	...	...	...	...
Solomon Islands	...	...	...	...	...	...	...
Vanuatu	...	...	...	...	...	...	...
Developed (Industrialized) Economies							
Australia	>95	>95	>95	>95	>95	>95	>95
Japan	>95	>95	>95	>95	>95	>95	>95
New Zealand	>95	>95	>95	>95	>95	>95	>95

Note. Timor-Leste: On May 20, 2002, Timor Leste became an independent country.
Data for Indonesia include Timor-Leste through 1999 unless otherwise noted.

Source: World Bank, *World Development Indicators,* WDI on-line, 25 January 2005.

Table V.4.1. Educational attainment of adult population 1985, 1990, 1995, 2000

(average years of schooling, population ages 15 and over)

	1985	1990	1995	2000
East Asia				
China	4.9	5.9	6.1	6.4
Korea, Rep. of	8.7	9.9	10.6	10.8
Mongolia	...	...	...	...
South-East Asia				
Cambodia	...	...	...	...
Indonesia	4.0	4.0	4.6	5.0
Lao PDR	...	...	...	...
Malaysia	5.5	6.0	6.5	6.8
Myanmar	2.4	2.5	2.6	2.8
Philippines	6.7	7.3	7.9	8.2
Singapore	6.1	6.0	6.7	7.1
Timor-Leste	...	...	...	...
Thailand	5.2	5.6	6.1	6.5
Viet Nam	...	3.8	...	...
South Asia				
Afghanistan	1.3	1.3	1.5	1.7
Bangladesh	2.1	2.2	2.4	2.6
India	3.6	4.1	4.5	5.1
Iran, Islamic Rep. of	3.4	4.0	4.7	5.3
Nepal	1.2	1.6	2.0	2.4
Pakistan	2.1	4.2	3.9	3.9
Sri Lanka	5.9	6.1	6.5	6.9
Pacific Islands				
Fiji	7.5	7.9	8.1	8.3
Kiribati	...	...	...	...
Papua New Guinea	2.0	2.3	2.6	2.9
Solomon Islands	...	...	...	...
Vanuatu	...	...	...	...
Developed (Industrialized) Economies				
Australia	10.3	10.4	10.7	10.9
Japan	8.7	9.0	9.2	9.5
New Zealand	11.5	11.3	11.5	11.7

Source: Barro, Robert J. and Jong-Wha Lee, *International Data on Educational Attainment: Updates and Implications* (CID Working Paper no. 42), Center for International Development at Harvard University, April 2000.